WINDOWBOX
GARDENING

WINDOWBOX GARDENING

DAVID JOYCE

The
Globe
Pequot
Press

Old Saybrook, Connecticut

TO BETTY

This American edition first published by
The Globe Pequot Press
Old Saybrook, Connecticut 06475

First published in Great Britain in 1993 by
Conran Octopus Limited
37 Shelton Street
London WC2H 9HN

Library of Congress Cataloging-in-Publication Data
Joyce, David.
    Windowbox gardening / David Joyce. — 1st American
    ed.
        p.   cm.
    Includes index.
    ISBN 1-56440-292-4
    1. Container gardening. 2. Window gardening. I. Title.
SB418.J695   1993
635.9'86—dc20
                                    93-4721
                                    CIP

Special projects photographed by Pia Tryde
Styling and assistance by Juliette Wade
Typeset by Servis Filmsetting Limited, Manchester
Printed and bound in Hong Kong

First Globe Pequot Edition/First Printing.

CONTENTS

INTRODUCTION

The idea of decorating the exteriors of buildings with containers of plants is a very old one indeed. In our own time, however, its appeal has taken off. A simple explanation for this lies in the fact that so many of us live in towns and cities, where a sill, balcony or small paved yard may be the only available gardening space. What is astonishing is that so many gardeners transcend the limitations of space in satisfying their urge to cultivate and to make where they live or work a more pleasant place to be.

The approach to this type of gardening varies greatly from one situation to another. If a simple windowbox has to suffice it can become a garden in itself, an intimate expression of its creator's personality. The view of it that counts is from inside the building. A collection of favorite plants might frame a pleasant outlook or mask an unattractive one. Dressing a house from the outside is the extrovert's approach. The result can be beautiful when a house is enhanced by a coordinated scheme or when mundane buildings are luxuriantly clothed with plants.

ABOVE: Wall-trained clematis mingles with a windowbox of pelargoniums. OPPOSITE: Windowboxes of matched flowers and foliage, with wall-trained wisteria and roses, make a lavish supplement to a narrow front garden.

The aim of this book is to present clear information on window gardening that will encourage and inspire the faint-hearted and the total beginner alike, and at the same time suggest ideas that might be new to the experienced gardener. I have used here the expression 'window gardening' because the scope of this book goes beyond straightforward windowboxes. It is true that windowboxes provide the simplest way to grow plants when the only space available is the windowsill of a flat, and they also offer the best means of carrying out ambitious schemes to dress the front of a house; but other containers, improvised as well as purpose-made, have their uses and can be displayed in a variety of interesting ways. Sometimes containers on sills are not practical: sills may not be deep enough or windows may open outwards. Stands or staging housing collections of pots may then be the answer, positioned either beneath a window or so that a collection of plants forms the focal point of a view from inside the house. Many points made in this book are applicable to such container gardening.

Plant Repertoire

For real dash and zest, window gardening is hard to beat. It offers a wonderful chance to test several design options and experiment with a wide range of plants in a way that makes borders look static and staid. Naturally the location imposes certain limitations. Plants much more than 2ft/60cm tall are likely to be unstable on windowsills, and in any case large plants will cut out light and block views. Size is not such a critical factor for container-grown plants placed on staging or at ground level on terraces and patios, but when choosing plants for these positions it is still important to take height and proportion into account.

Even allowing for size constraints, there is a rich resource of plants to draw on. Those listed in the Plant Guide (pages 72–89) will satisfy many readers but adventurous gardeners will find plenty of others with which to experiment. Ensuring that plants will look well together should be the overriding consideration when making a selection. The approach can be much less conventional than is normally the case in the open garden. In summer schemes hardy plants might be combined with tender ones borrowed from the greenhouse or the house. Long-lived plants such as herbaceous perennials and even shrubs can be used extravagantly, as if they were short-term plants. Suggestions for combining plants in different ways are provided under relevant headings later in the book. As a general point, however, it is worth noting here that the best effects are generally achieved when plants of different habit are brought together: trailers to mask the hard edges of containers combined with more upright plants, for example, or loose-limbed sprawlers with plants that are dense and bushy. Getting the mixture right is particularly important with windowboxes, and the longer the container the more difficult it is to counteract its rigidly horizontal format.

LEFT: Tall-growing tulips are often blown over or damaged by wind. For windowboxes it is best to choose from among the many early-flowering short-stemmed kinds, mainly hybrids of Tulipa fosteriana, T. greigii, *and* T. kaufmanniana.

OPPOSITE: Plants that combine good foliage and attractive flowers are invaluable. The ivy-leaved pelargoniums trail elegantly, have handsome leaves and flower throughout summer.

Aspect

Two factors that are sometimes overlooked have an important bearing on the choice of plants for a window garden. While most medium-sized gardens offer a number of protected niches, the exposure of a window garden to sun and wind is determined largely by the orientation of a building. Planting must therefore be adapted to suit the conditions.

The first image conjured up by the word 'windowbox' is of a bright, flowery mass spilling from a sunny sill. The potency of this image owes much to a relatively small group of widely planted sun-lovers that flower prolifically over a long summer season. Petunias, pelargoniums, verbenas and the like are extremely useful, as are foliage plants such as *Helichrysum petiolare* that are often mixed with them. It is a shame, though, that so much reliance is placed on a narrow band of plants when there are so many good sun-lovers that do well in windowboxes and other containers. It is as well to be aware, however, that some plants take sun-loving to extremes, their

flowers remaining closed in dull weather and opening only for part of the day, even in bright weather. Light metering is most evident in several of the South African daisy flowers, including arctotis, gazanias, mesembryanthemums and osteospermums. In late winter or early spring, crocuses also need warmth or light to spread their petals.

Many of the true shade-lovers are woodland plants, and most of these thrive in dappled light filtered through a canopy of deciduous foliage. Such broken shade is uncommon close to buildings. Depending on the aspect, conditions can vary between full sun and permanent shade, but it is true to say that most walls are sunny for part of the day and shady for the rest, the proportion of sun to shade changing with the seasons. The densest shade is often found where walls hem in a window to form a narrow yard. Painting the walls white or off-white improves light levels and flatters plants, especially foliage.

Most plants that are happiest in dappled shade can tolerate the cruder distribution of light and shade close to buildings. In spring, plants such as primroses and polyanthus (*Primula*) will flower freely in moderate shade, and yellow daffodils make a cheerful sunny impression. Lack of sun will tend to make them droop but they can be moved on before their untidiness becomes too bothersome.

In deep shade the sun-lovers of summer will also become lanky and many will flower only sparingly. But provided they get four or five

LEFT: *Impatiens are among the most reliable summer flowers for a windowbox in part shade.*

OPPOSITE: *A sunny balcony dazzles with red pelargoniums and white petunias.*

hours of sun a day, some, including petunias and nasturtiums, will flower reasonably well. The more time they spend in the shade, the more leaf they produce, and the result may be lovely foliage with an occasional flower. If displays including sun-lovers are planted in movable containers they can be mounted in shade provided that from time to time they are allowed a day or two to bask in the sun.

Clippings from the sunny garden are a useful supplement to a summer display of shade-tolerant plants such as busy Lizzies, pansies or violas. But the real stars of the shade garden are some fine foliage plants and a few flowering shrubs, of which rhododendrons are outstanding. A scheme combining the delicate patterns of fern fronds with the bold outlines of bergenias and hostas, as on pages 68—9, can form the basis of a sophisticated display.

Wind is the scourge of the window garden. Shrieking winter gales and summer storms can be disastrous, but even in relatively calm weather, upper windowsills can be buffeted so violently as to dislodge inadequately secured containers. Wind can cruelly damage brittle and flimsy plants. It is also desiccating; the windier the conditions, the more watering plants will need.

Naturals for exposed positions are perennials and shrubs that have made adaptations to harsh conditions, as have many of the rock-garden plants suitable for the alpine trough on pages 46—7. These are usually compact, often ground-hugging, and they have developed their own defense mechanisms against desiccation and drought, including small, leathery, fleshy or hairy leaves.

Although they are often used excessively in the open garden, dwarf annuals and bedding

plants are among the successes of plant breeding. Examples ideal for windowboxes include the short-growing antirrhinums, wallflowers and tobacco plants, whose stockiness is ample compensation for the loss of attractive proportions. (Miniature daffodils are in fact a return to the original proportions of the species.) By planting short-growing cultivars and smaller-flowered kinds, the risk of wind damage can be minimized. It also helps to plant densely to a fairly uniform height so that the plants themselves are able to support each other. Where strong winds are a known factor, avoid fragile plants such as tuberous begonias, dahlias and fuchsias.

SILLS FOR STYLE Rustic

or sophisticated, the choice of plants and containers can help to create a distinctive style

If you are using windowboxes to dress a house, it is often helpful to plan a planting scheme in terms of a particular style. Admittedly 'style' is a rather inflated term to apply to many of the modest schemes that are a source of pleasure to gardeners and passers-by. It is important, however, to think through the effect that you wish to achieve, and having a style or theme in mind makes this much easier. If you do not already have windowboxes, consider the effect you wish to achieve before buying. Simple containers that can easily be adapted to suit different styles are often the best choice.

Often the most appropriate course is to take your cue from the architecture. The best way of treating a house with a symmetrical front, classical or modern, may be to style windowboxes in a formal way, echoing the balance of the architecture in the arrangement of containers and also in the planting within the containers. For a simple house in the country, a cottage garden style might be the best

ABOVE: Pots of familiar spring flowers suggest a cottage garden.
OPPOSITE: The climber Parthenocissus tricuspidata *and windowboxes of pink petunias make a handsome decoration for a dignified rustic house.*

approach. However, many window gardeners live in suburban houses or in urban apartments. The building may not itself suggest a particular style or theme – and it may be better to ignore or disguise it rather than seek to flatter it.

Three styles are discussed here – formal, cottage and Mediterranean – but they incorporate ideas that can be adapted or elaborated according to personal preference and the conditions in which you garden. You might opt for a tropical effect, in which lush vegetation is combined with exotic flowers. Even in temperate regions of the world this is possible in summer by borrowing tender plants from the greenhouse or house. Another possibility is a desert theme, based on a display of prickly cacti and other succulents. In many temperate regions this would only be suitable as a summer display. Bonsai, plants miniaturized by careful pruning and cultivation, are an obvious choice for an Oriental theme but are better suited to a staged display than a windowbox or container arrangement on a sill.

Formal Style

It was an axiom of the nineteenth-century landscapists, often repeated since, that the nearer the garden is to the house the more formal it should be. On the face of it, there is a good case for treating formally a garden close to a building, particularly if the architecture of the building itself is symmetrical or classical. By the same token, matched windowboxes and matched plantings can reinforce the symmetry of a house. And the symmetry can be extended to the arrangement within each box by placing the largest plant centrally and flanking it with identical groups of plants on either side. Using plants of very clear, simple shapes underlines the formality of such schemes. The most regular shapes are those imposed by trimming, as with geometric topiary specimens. Box (*Buxus sempervirens*) is the most suitable topiary plant for window gardens, and simple balls, cones and pyramids of less than 2ft/60cm will, with a trim once a year, hold their shape more or less indefinitely. Geometric shapes can also

OPPOSITE: The formality of this rich but ordered display relies on its symmetrical arrangement and on the repetition of the planting in troughs attached to the foreground railings.

*ABOVE LEFT: Simple geometric topiary immediately strikes a formal note. A ball of clipped box (*Buxus sempervirens*) is here flanked in spring by grape hyacinths (*Muscari*).*

ABOVE RIGHT: A highly decorative ironwork grille for a windowbox makes a pleasing contrast to the stately, upright growth of spring Narcissi.

be formed by training ivy on simple frames, although these need to be well anchored so that they don't tip.

The combination of regular shapes and symmetry can be very severe, and it helps to have loose, trailing plants breaking the edge of windowboxes and hinting at the possibility of disorder. It is generally a mistake to soften the effect of a formal scheme by using a decorated container. Many modern windowboxes are fussily ornamented with debased versions of traditional decoration, and you are much better off with something plain.

Cottage Style

ABOVE: Small-flowered petunias in a narrow color range complement the cottage-garden plants growing in a border against this clapboard house.

OPPOSITE: Plump mounds of busy Lizzies and purple lobelia, surrounded by a mature wisteria, are a suitably pretty adornment for this Gothic-style window.

The term 'cottage style' can be used to describe an informal scheme in which plants appear to have been brought together almost randomly. In the spirit of a true cottage garden, useful herbs and attractive ornamentals can find themselves side by side in the same box, the assumption being that plants will simply rub along with one another in an amicable sort of way.

There are, however, pitfalls. The old-fashioned flowers of the traditional cottage garden were not the brash, showy things that plant breeders have since produced for us. They blended well together because they were not all clamoring for attention in the way many of the large highly-colored modern cultivars do. A purely random mixture of these new varieties in the reduced compass of a window-box can make for a very discordant effect that has little to do with true cottage style. If you are using heavily-built modern cultivars in strong colors then it is as well to choose flowers and foliage that complement each other, as suggested in Color Choice.

A reasonably authentic cottage style can, however, be very attractive on a simple country house and can be easily adapted to almost any setting. In order to achieve it you will need some old-fashioned flowers. There is greatly renewed interest in the genuine old cultivars and also in new cultivars that are close to them in character. There are good examples among pinks (*Dianthus*) and primroses (*Primula*). Double and gold-laced primroses rather than the beefy modern polyanthus can be used for spring schemes with miniature bulbs; so, too, can double forms of the annual daisy (*Bellis perennis*) and celandine (*Ranunculus ficaria*). A summer planting could include pansies and the similar but smaller-flowered violas, pinks (the old kinds include many that are beautifully fringed and laced, some of them strongly clove-scented), and, for hotter colors, pot marigolds (*Calendula*) and nasturtiums (*Tropaeolum*). Simple wooden windowboxes are appropriate for a cottage garden scheme, but a collection of improvised containers can be equally effective (see pages 58–9).

Mediterranean Style

Even in regions where the summer is not reliably sunny, the languorous heat of Mediterranean countries can be evoked by colorful windowboxes. To my way of thinking, schemes that set out to achieve this effect should be simple collections of colorful flowers, not carefully elaborated plantings that rely on subtle pastels. It is difficult to better the pelargoniums in this respect. The ivy-leaved kinds have the advantage of combining in the one plant good foliage and attractive flowers. A sunny house front decorated with several boxes planted up with the same cultivar can be highly effective. Good companions are pot-grown specimens of Mediterranean plants such as oleanders (*Nerium oleander*) and citrus trees, plants that in cool, temperate regions will need winter protection. A wall-trained grapevine provides an authentic backdrop and, where the climate allows, warmth-loving climbers such as bougainvillea and the trumpet vine (*Campsis*) can be added to it. The most appropriate material for a Mediterranean-style windowbox is terracotta, but it is worth remembering that a skirt of ivy-leaved pelargoniums will hide almost any container. Also in keeping with the style are improvisations, including plants in painted tins.

LEFT: *Even a shady doorway would be lit by the red glow of these impatiens. There is a casual confidence in the way the pots are hung from the bracket and door grille and are held in the old stand.*

OPPOSITE: *Tiers of pelargoniums in shades of red and pink arranged on the façade wreathed in grapevine and plumbago contribute to an authentically Mediterranean combination.*

Hanging Buckets

Improvisation is in the true spirit of the cottage garden, where making do has often been an economic necessity. Using old-fashioned domestic receptacles as plant containers can help create an impression of simple rusticity. When planted with a froth of tumbling flowers, galvanized buckets lose their associations with dreary, mundane chores. They are just as attractive bearing crops of strawberries or trailing cherry tomatoes and fully in keeping with a cottage style, in which there is no sharp division between useful and ornamental plants.

A row of buckets hung from beneath a windowsill is a very pretty alternative to a windowbox. Once filled with moist compost and plants, the buckets will be heavy, so for safety they must be attached by sturdy hooks to a firm sill or bracket. The handle clearance will limit to some extent the choice of plants.

YOU WILL NEED:
3 galvanized buckets, approximately 2 gallons/9 litres capacity
Broken crocks or other drainage material
Approximately 4½ gallons/20 litres potting compost
Strong hooks to hold the buckets

3 ornamental cabbages
3 *Convolvulus sabatius*
3 *Diascia*
3 *Pentas lanceolata*
3 *Sedum* 'Vera Jameson'

1. Drill three or four drainage holes in the bottom of each bucket. On a wooden sill, fix sturdy hooks to the underside, spaced equally to allow for the bucket handles.
2. Put a layer of old crocks or similar material in the bottom of each bucket for drainage. Fill most of the bucket with compost.
3. Knock the plants out of their pots and plant them up. Divide them equally between the buckets, but change the configuration each time. Fill around the plants with compost, water the buckets well, and hang them up.

DECORATIVE CONTAINERS

Whether purpose-made or improvised, containers can be subordinate to a planting scheme or highly decorative

There are two basic requirements that all plant containers must satisfy. They must be of sufficient size to hold enough compost to meet the needs of plants. If there is not enough compost, plants will not have a firm anchor, and the supply of water and nutrients will be exhausted too rapidly. The containers must also have drainage holes. Plants need air as well as water at their roots, and in stagnant, wet compost most plants will eventually drown. If there are too many drainage holes the compost may escape and, even if it is held in place, is likely to dry out too quickly.

All containers that are purpose-built for growing plants, including windowboxes, pots and tubs, should have an adequate number of drainage holes of the right size. However, poor finish often means that holes are partially or fully blocked. Check before using containers and clear holes if necessary. Drainage is often impeded when containers sit flat on a surface. Unless pots and windowboxes have built-in feet or a ridged base, raise them slightly using

ABOVE: An uncomplicated decoration, such as fluting, can enhance the appeal of a terracotta windowbox.
OPPOSITE: This simple planting of impatiens allows the decorative wirework of the baskets to be seen.

purpose-built supports or blocks of wood so that they sit about 1in/2.5cm above the sill. If a shallow drip tray is used to prevent staining and possible damage to the sill, the feet should hold the box so that its base is at a higher level than the rim of the tray to ensure that plants do not stand in waterlogged soil.

It is often easy enough to drill holes in the base of improvised wooden and metal containers such as old buckets, tins and kitchen utensils. Make sure that holes in metal containers are at the lowest point in the base so that drainage is not impeded. If a container such as a basket is too gappy it can be lined with polythene, provided that holes are slashed in the base to provide drainage. There are, however, many potential containers in which it is not possible or desirable to drill holes, and the best way to use these is as temporary holders for plastic pots that are dropped inside. When a decorative receptacle is used in this way, make sure that excess water is not allowed to collect in the base.

Container Choice

Many gardeners consider terracotta to be the only appropriate material for containers, and I agree that it is hard to improve on simple terracotta pots and windowboxes that allow you to focus attention on the plant. They are readily available in a wide range of sizes. Shallow terracotta pans about 4in/10cm deep are particularly useful for growing dwarf bulbs. Tall pots, 9in/23cm or more in height, are suitable for trailers. The weight of such containers can be a problem on roofs and balconies but in most situations their stability is a more significant factor. Weathered terracotta looks attractive, and the aging process can be speeded up by painting pots with a solution of organic manure or even a wash made with diluted plain yogurt.

One disadvantage of terracotta is that in hot weather it dries out fairly quickly. Water loss can be reduced by lining pots with black polythene, which must, of course, be slit at the base to allow free drainage. An additional drawback of much of the terracotta imported into cool, temperate regions from Mediterranean and tropical countries is that it is not frost-resistant.

Another traditional material, especially for windowboxes, is wood, and those who have the necessary skills can easily tailor-make wooden boxes to fit a sill. It is relatively easy,

TOP: *An old Coca-Cola box makes an attractive improvised container for pots of daffodils.*

LEFT: *Terracotta can be lightly colored to enhance its decorative effect.*

OPPOSITE: *Wall-mounting of windowboxes is a solution when sills are narrow.*

too, to attach a wooden box to the window surround so that there is no risk of it being dislodged. Wood needs to be treated with a preservative, such as one of the proprietary brands containing copper naphthenate, which is not harmful to plants. Never use creosote. Wooden windowboxes can be quickly painted to match or contrast with architectural features or, more adventurously, to complement the colors of a planting scheme.

Purists shudder at the thought of displaying plants in plastic containers, but these do have two significant advantages: they are readily available in a wide range of sizes and colors and are relatively inexpensive. Their lightness can be an asset too, as for example when a trough is supported by brackets beneath a window, though this can also be a disadvantage. Plants grown in plastic pots are easily blown over, especially when the compost used is a lightweight soilless one. My own view is that simple plastic pots and boxes are much less offensive to look at than many elaborately decorated containers. Windowboxes are often almost obscured by trailing plants, and dark pots with a mat finish often go unnoticed. The chief use of plastic containers, however, is for growing plants that are to be displayed temporarily in other receptacles; the plastic pot or windowbox liner should fit fairly snugly inside, with its rim just below that of the outer container.

Other materials widely used in the manufacture of containers include concrete and fiberglass. Concrete is heavy and looks raw at first, but it weathers well and can sometimes resemble stone. Fiberglass is lightweight and is often used to imitate other materials. Antique lead troughs are themselves prohibitively expensive, but imitations in fiberglass are

cheaper and can be very convincing.

Getting the size of the container right is not only important aesthetically but will also ensure the health of plants. If containers are too large the plants will look lost, but in containers that are too small water and nutrients are quickly used up. Plants that manage to survive in these conditions are usually miserable root-bound specimens. Windowboxes less than 6in/15cm wide and 8in/20cm deep are rarely satisfactory, and, ideally, boxes should fit fairly exactly the width of the sill.

Arranging and Improvising Containers

Windowboxes often play no part in the most imaginative of window gardens. The easiest way to display plants in their prime is to bring out a succession of pot-grown specimens from a greenhouse as they reach their peak and replace them as they go over. A program stage-managed with style can provide a sequence of splendid seasonal climaxes.

Another inventive approach to decorative gardening, which lies somewhere between conventional gardening and flower arranging, exploits the full ornamental value of containers as well as plants. At one extreme the results can be grotesquely self-conscious. At its best, however, executed with a flair for recognizing the ornamental quality in unusual or everyday containers, it is a wonderfully refreshing way of making plants part of daily living. It is often best to allow plants in highly decorated containers to play a subordinate role. Simple foliage, such as the undulating, strap-like leaves of hart's tongue fern (*Phyllitis scolopendrium*) or the black, spider-like leaves of *Ophiopogon planiscapus nigrescens*, may be much more suitable than showy flowers.

For the keen decorator the real excitement comes from searching out less conventional purpose-made containers and improvising from a vast range of receptacles of convenient

LEFT: Height variations can often be more easily achieved with a group of well-chosen containers than with a single windowbox.

OPPOSITE, LEFT: Ivy-leaved pelargoniums and a selection of other plants cascade from a windowbox and bracket containers.

OPPOSITE, RIGHT: White pansies stand out above a cluster of terracotta pots painted pink and blue.

size. Buckets and pails, old china pots from the kitchen and miscellaneous items from farm and workshop can all be pressed into service. The really mundane, such as old tins, can be transformed by a coat of paint chosen to match or contrast with their setting or, alternatively, the colors of the plants they are to contain.

A windowsill of cheerful plants in an almost random assembly of pots, a sort of Mediterranean medley, is difficult to beat for simple charm. It is most practical at a ground-floor window where no great danger is caused by a pot being dislodged, and where containers can easily be moved if necessary. A pot-holding bracket is a useful precaution even at ground-floor level, and essential at upper windows where pots can cause injury if they fall. If it is possible to get a drip tray the same dimensions as the sill, so much the better, but it should be emptied if it fills with rain water.

A limitation of the windowbox is that it presents a uniform horizontal line. An escape from this tyranny is to use one or two large containers with a clustering entourage of smaller ones, for example flanking a windowbox by two tall pots or placing a large container between two small windowboxes.

Often, however, sills are not wide enough to take pots of reasonable size, or windows open outwards, making it inconvenient to have an encumbered sill. The stands and staging that were much used for the display of plants in Victorian times are regaining popularity and are often the best means of displaying container-grown plants at a window. One type, consisting of a long, narrow basket of open wirework supported on wrought-iron legs about 30in/75cm high, is designed to sit under a window. More complicated designs consist of three or more levels of staging, narrower at the top than at the bottom. Most of these are meant to stand against a wall, and one of the most attractive ways of using them is as the focal point of a view from the house. The period flavor of this kind of staging can be very appealing but something just as effective can be made using planks supported by upturned flowerpots or stacks of bricks.

Baskets of Roses

6 argyranthemums
6 'patio' or other appropriate roses

1. Assemble all the ingredients.
2. To prolong the life of the basket, treat it with at least two coats of yacht varnish, working it well into the weave. Allow to dry thoroughly.
3. Cut from a sheet of polythene a generous liner and, before laying it in position, cut slits in the base for drainage.
4. Put in drainage material to a depth of 1–2in/2.5–5cm before filling with compost and planting with roses.

Beautifully textured and freely available in a wide range of shapes and sizes, wicker baskets can easily be converted into appealing plant containers. Pink 'patio' roses make the ideal partners.

For two wicker baskets, approximately 20in/50cm × 12in/30cm in length and breadth by 10in/25cm deep, you will need:
0.44 pint/250ml yacht varnish
1 stiff brush
Black or clear polythene sheet approximately 83in/ 210cm × 65in/165cm
1 quart/1 litre coarse shingle or other drainage material
2 gallons/10 litres loam-based potting compost
trowel

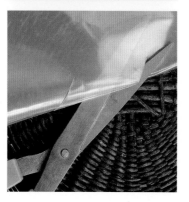

SHORT-TERM SCHEMES

For seasonal impact, capturing spring's freshness or the opulence of summer, plant two or more schemes a year

Replanting windowboxes during the year offers the best chance of sustaining lively and colorful displays. For those who do not have the necessary space to hold plants in reserve, the simplest course is to make two changes a year. For a summer display, plant in late spring. Nurseries and garden centers often have specimens available earlier, but there is a risk that half-hardy plants will be damaged by frost if planted prematurely. The effectiveness of the summer display depends on using plants that perform well over an extended season. There are many to choose from that flower throughout the summer, often until the first frosts. In autumn, when their show is over, these plants should be lifted and disposed of and replaced by others for a spring display.

Increasing the number of changes a year makes for more interesting gardening, but re-planting directly in windowboxes can result in irregular growth patterns. It is enormously useful to have rigid, lightweight windowbox liners that can be planted up in a holding

ABOVE: Petunias are standbys for summer, flowering prolifically over a long season.
OPPOSITE: A gap in a garden wall holds a summer mixture of pink pelargoniums, impatiens and boldly marked monkey flowers (Mimulus).

station so that as one display fades, another is ready to take its place. There may be enough storage room for this on a balcony, but clearly those with a garden and, even better, a greenhouse, have an advantage: flowers for early summer, when there is often a lull after the spring display, can be brought on inside and then hardened off before being planted in a windowbox.

There is no point in being over-scrupulous about the kinds of plants you use for short-term schemes. On the small scale of a window garden hardy herbaceous perennials and shrubs can be used for effect in the same way as you might use annuals and biennials. Consider it a bonus if they can be salvaged when a display comes to an end. The greenhouse or house can also provide plants that will be happy enough outdoors in summer. Rex begonias and coleus (*Solenostemon*) will provide some of the richest foliage colors you can find, and trailers, like the variegated wandering Jew (*Tradescantia*), are invaluable.

Spring and Summer Schemes

If schemes are changed twice a year, providing spring and summer displays, as on pages 38–9, the plantings can be made directly into the windowbox. It does not matter whether the first planting takes place in autumn, when bulbs and other winter- or spring-flowering plants are put in, or in late spring, for the summer season. At the start of the cycle, begin with containers scrubbed clean, and use fresh soilless or loam-based compost. The compost can be used for one year but should be replaced at the beginning of the new cycle. When the windowboxes are emptied at the end of the cycle, take the opportunity to scrub them out before filling them with fresh compost. Also add fresh compost at the mid-cycle change-over, when some of the growing medium will inevitably be lost. Even with annual replacement of the soil, it is necessary to feed regularly during the summer months to sustain a good supply of nutrients and advisable to give a liquid feed once or twice in early and mid-spring, particularly if the autumn planting occurs in the middle of the cycle.

LEFT: For weather resistance, the short-stemmed early-flowering tulips are the most appropriate choice, but taller varieties make useful and attractive companions for grape hyacinths (Muscari) and other bulbs of mid- to late spring.

BELOW: The large-flowered or Dutch crocuses make a bold display in the middle of spring. Plant them densely and in layers for maximum impact.

OPPOSITE: Regular deadheading ensures that pansies give a long season. The winter-flowering kinds continue well into spring, and summer-flowering pansies can be brought on to flower in late spring.

For the summer display, heavy reliance is usually placed on a relatively small group of familiar plants that have a capacity to flower almost uninterruptedly from early summer until the first frosts. Lobelia, petunias, pelargoniums and the like provide a long season, and they are not plants to shun simply because of their popularity. The attention breeders have paid to them has resulted in a range of colors and forms that can be exploited in bold and subtle combinations. The wide choice avail-

ABOVE: Petunias, fuchsias and lobelia are free-flowering plants giving a long summer season. The combination has often been repeated but can be given fresh appeal if full use is made of the wide color range available.

OPPOSITE: A nasturtium (Tropaeolum majus) overflows from a flourishing summer windowbox that includes lobelia, pelargoniums and Tagetes, apparently changing flower color as it trickles into a display of container-grown plants stationed beneath the window.

able means that even with a relatively small selection of plants it is possible to present a different kind of display each year. If you are aiming for special effects, it may be necessary to raise your own plants from seed since nurseries and garden centers in general are not reliable sources of supply for the more unusual colors. There are, however, a number of less familiar plants with long flowering seasons. The daisy flowers of *Arctotis* and *Osteospermum*, the pink spires of diascias and the exquisite blue funnels of *Convolvulus sabatius* can all give summer-long pleasure.

Productive plants – annual herbs, vegetables and fruit – are other possibilities for summer windowboxes. The satisfaction of growing vegetables successfully has to be set against the small amount of produce a windowbox is likely to yield and the sometimes limited decorative value of edible plants.

Bulbs are the perfect choice for a spring explosion of color. I prefer to buy fresh stocks from dependable suppliers each year so that I can confidently expect a good display. However, it is usually worth saving bulbs when they are lifted after flowering, for planting out in the open garden. If you have no garden yourself, pass them on to friends who can enjoy them in subsequent years. First, grow them on in pots or in the open ground until the leaves die down; this will ensure a good flowering the following year. They can then be lifted and dried off for replanting in autumn.

Companions for, or alternatives to, bulbs include biennials, among them wallflowers and winter-flowering pansies. The pansies give exceptional value, coming into flower in winter and continuing through spring, sometimes even into summer.

Successional Planting

A pair of liners per windowbox should be enough to withstand the changes of four to five plants a year if they are lifted from liners and either discarded or planted in the garden as soon as their display is over. The same compost, either soilless or loam-based, can be used for two or three displays. Top with fresh compost at each changeover, and replace it completely at one point in the annual cycle. Before putting in new compost, clean the liners thoroughly.

Successional planting allows plenty of scope for a personal selection of plants, and inventive gardeners will be able to think of many variations on the following suggestions.

The flowering season of most bulbs is rarely more than three weeks, and this is a strong case in itself for having more than one spring scheme. You could start in late winter with a windowbox thickly planted with precocious early bulbs such as species crocuses, dwarf irises, puschkinia and snowdrops. Show them off against a glossy evergreen, a small-leaved ivy, for example. Daffodils and jonquils are the principal bulbs of mid-spring, followed only slightly later by hyacinths. Any of these bulbs can be combined with the double-flowered common daisy (*Bellis perennis*), winter-flowering pansies, which are fully into their stride by the spring, and polyanthus; alternatively these plants can be used together without any bulbs at all. The primrose (*Primula vulgaris*) and its various forms make lovely plants for the second half of spring and go well with small-flowered violas. Tulips reign supreme among the bulbs of late spring, and happily they coincide with richly scented wallflowers (*Cheiranthus cheiri*) and the hazy blue of forget-me-nots (*Myosotis*).

Summer may be divided into two halves, starting with a planting dominated by hardy

annuals such as Californian poppies (*Eschscholzia*), which have been sown early in the year or the preceding summer. Have a liner planted with half-hardy or tender replacements to take over when the first team's profuse flowering begins to falter. Tuberous begonias, dwarf dahlias and fuchsias, as well as the invaluable foliage plant *Helichrysum petiolare*, are all good plants for the second half of summer.

For the period between early autumn and late winter there is a limited range of short-term ornamentals, and shrubby and herbaceous plants are often called in to fill the gap. The winter-flowering heathers can be added to permanent plantings of shrubs to give winter color, or they can just as easily be treated as short-term plants on their own or combined with an evergreen perennial. Bergenias, with their unusual and varied winter colors, make a welcome alternative to dwarf conifers. Among my favorites for autumn and winter are the ornamental cabbages, their large leaf rosettes often beautifully patterned in glaucous green, pink, and creamy white.

OPPOSITE: Pots of daisies and double primroses combined with early violas are useful and attractive alternatives to, or companions for, bulbs in the second half of spring.

RIGHT: In mild areas, the hybrid rhododendrons (azaleas), commonly sold as houseplants, can make a vivid display during late winter.

BELOW: Many professionals use a core of evergreens for a period of six months or a year, adding other plants seasonally every two or three months. Florists' cyclamen, here taking over from heathers, are useful in mild areas for a late autumn display.

A Summer Trough

1. Lay out newspaper or a polythene sheet for discarded plants, and assemble materials for the new planting. Lift plants that are to be replaced, and shake lightly to minimize loss of compost.
2. Loosen the compost left in the trough, mixing fresh compost with it.
3. Replant for summer, creating a balance between bushy and trailing plants. Water the newly planted container thoroughly.

By early summer at the latest it is time to replace a winter scheme with fresh plants that will give a long display. With two changes in an annual cycle the compost needs to be replaced once a year. The trough is here being replanted for summer in mid-cycle.

For a low window without a sill, a raised trough is often a convenient solution.

YOU WILL NEED:
A raised wooden trough, height (with legs) 2ft/60cm, depth 1ft/30cm, length 3ft/90cm, width 14in/36cm
About 1 gallon/4.5 litres soilless potting compost
Trowel

2 *Heuchera micrantha* 'Palace Purple'
6 mixed osteospermums
4 pink-flowered verbenas

LONG-TERM SCHEMES

Plant evergreens for continuity, and for variety add seasonal plants that can be replaced once they are over

The principal aim of many long-term plantings is to dress a house or apartment so that it has a settled feeling to it. Evergreen shrubs are the easiest plants to use to create this effect. A familiar combination is a conifer with swags of ivy; whether that is a classic or a cliché depends on your point of view.

Another reason that gardeners sometimes opt for the long-term solution is to save labor, but the most time-consuming task in maintaining a windowbox is not in fact replanting but watering. Shrubs and other long-term plants may not collapse immediately if left unwatered, but they do not stand much chance of surviving if they are neglected for days or weeks at a time between spring and autumn. The use of a mulch will slow down water loss but is not a substitute for regular watering. There is no room for benign neglect. If long-term plants are not properly cared for, they will suffer and eventually die.

Although some evergreens have flowers and berries that add seasonal touches, many remain

ABOVE: Trailing ivy and dwarf or slow-growing conifers make a simple, dignified combination.
OPPOSITE: Mophead hydrangeas used as long-term plants are in keeping with the scale of this trough and stone-built house.

relatively static throughout the year, giving little impression of the changing seasons. Long-term schemes can, however, be brightened up with seasonal plants. The long-term component might be no more than a single key plant, such as a specimen of geometric topiary, but bulbs can be added for spring color and plants with a prolonged flowering season for summer. In effect this program is an adaptation of two-phase short-term schemes, but with an element that remains constant.

A very different kind of long-term planting is one that is much less concerned with the outsider's view of a building. Its aim is to create a long-term miniature garden, and the most suitable plants to achieve this are the dwarf shrubs and perennials usually grown in rock gardens. While you will not get festoons of profusely flowering annuals, you can expect to achieve a succession of quite exquisite seasonal performances, from delicate spring bulbs to the charming flowers of gentians or even miniature thymes.

Sustaining the Display

There are many compact evergreens for sun or shade that can be used as key plants to ensure that a windowbox planting holds up throughout the year. The scope is greatly extended if your window garden can include large tubs or pots clustered in a yard, on a patio or balcony or arranged on staging, for then you can use plants that would be too large for growing on sills. Flowering evergreens, as has been suggested, give a sense of the changing seasons, and their floral display can sometimes last several weeks. There is a role for deciduous shrubs as well; after all, many are superb flowering and foliage plants. However, their best use in long-term planting schemes is as subordinates rather than key plants.

The range of annuals and bedding plants that flower freely in shade is limited, and a long-term planting in which the key plant or plants are flowering shrubs is often a good solution for a windowbox in such a position. The dwarf rhododendrons can be truly spectacular, and

OPPOSITE: The most suitable roses for windowboxes are miniatures or the slightly larger 'patio' roses. On a balcony there is room for larger repeat-flowering bush roses.

ABOVE, LEFT: A bright display of spring flowers supplements a core planting of Viburnum tinus *and* Leucothoë *'Scarletta'.*

ABOVE, RIGHT: The effect of long-term planting can be enhanced by a sprinkling of seasonal additions. Here tuberous begonias peep out from hebes and variegated euonymus.

they do well in light shade provided they are grown in a lime-free compost that is kept moist. Their companions should be plants that like the same sort of compost and conditions. The gaultherias are lovers of moist, acidic soil, and these are among the best of the evergreens that carry winter berries.

Most herbaceous perennials are deciduous and can leave awkward gaps in winter. If you have a garden to plunder you could treat them purely as short-term additions for the summer. There are, however, some good perennials that hold their leaves through the winter.

Ground-covering bugle (*Ajuga reptans*) has attractive purple-leaved and variegated forms and, as a bonus, spikes of blue flowers in spring. A really striking plant in bronzy purple is *Heuchera micrantha* 'Palace Purple', which is large enough to displace shrubs as the dominant plant.

The kind of long-term scheme shown on pages 46–7 is for the gardener who delights in the detail of plants. The dwarf shrubs and perennials that are suitable for this, some but not all of them alpines, are compact plants whose growth habit is a response to a harsh and windswept natural environment. They need sun but most do well in exposed positions and many are remarkably tolerant of drought. The main problem they pose is that so many flower in late spring and early summer. It helps to include a few good foliage plants, such as dwarf conifers and the rosette-forming sempervivums, in order to give background shape to the planting scheme and interest throughout the year, while early crocuses and other small bulbs and late-flowering plants (dwarf campanulas are a good choice) help to extend the flower display.

With all long-term schemes use a loam-based compost, which should be rejuvenated annually. If you plan to supplement seasonally the display provided by key long-term plants, the calendar is the same as for two-phase short-

*LEFT: Its numerous variations in leaf shape and color, its decorative qualities, trailing habit and toughness, all make the common ivy (*Hedera helix*) an invaluable long-term plant for windowboxes and containers of all kinds. It is a perfect companion for fuchsias in summer.*

term schemes: plant bulbs and other spring flowers in autumn, lift and replace them with summer-flowering plants in late spring, and complete the cycle by lifting and replacing these when they die in autumn. Top with fresh compost at each phase of the cycle, and apply a liquid fertilizer to short-term plants during the summer.

ABOVE: The variegated forms of ivy are particularly useful in winter, their color brightening a somber season. In this trough mounted on railings, cyclamen has been added to a long-term planting scheme that includes skimmias, spotted laurel (a cultivar of Aucuba japonica) *and a conifer.*

An Alpine Trough

The exquisite forms and flowers of rock-garden and alpine plants are ideal for a miniature long-term garden in a trough or windowbox.

YOU WILL NEED:
1 terracotta trough, 2ft/60cm long, 12in/30cm wide and 10in/25cm high
Clay pellets or other drainage material
2 gallons/10 litres loam-based potting compost
1 quart/1 litre horticultural grit or silver sand
1 quart/1 litre stone chippings
Trowel or handfork

2 *Arabis ferdinandi-coburgii* 'Variegata'
2 *Chrysanthemopsis hosmariense*
1 *Helianthemum* 'The Bride'

1 *Picea mariana* 'Nana'
1 *Raoulia hookeri*
1 *Sedum spathulifolium* 'Purpureum'
1 *Sempervivum* 'Cleveland Morgan'
2 *Thymus richardii* ssp. *nitidus* 'Peter Davis'
1 *Thymus serpyllum coccineus*

1. In the base of the trough, place a layer of drainage material about 2in/5cm deep. Good drainage is essential for alpine plants.
2. Mix sand or horticultural grit with the compost to make a free-draining mixture.
3. Start planting by positioning a key specimen.
4. Spread a surface layer of stone chippings about ½in/7.5mm deep before watering.

COLOR CHOICE

For gentle harmonies or striking contrasts, there are flower and foliage colors of every shade

For many gardeners, including myself, one of the greatest pleasures of combining plants on a small scale is making the most of a staggeringly complex palette of plant color. There is a school of thought that regards 'good taste' as achievable only through the rigorous vetting and coordination of flowers and foliage to create perfect harmonies of color. I favor a more relaxed approach that leaves room for experiment. Window gardening offers the possibility to experiment frequently. You might decide to group together colors that lie close to one another on the spectrum, such as brick reds and oranges, or to make the most of contrasts, for example combining blues and violets with yellows. Fortunately you do not have to live forever with your most original and exuberant schemes or with the results of careless whimsy. The edgy vibrancy of orange and purple, mauve and scarlet or yellow and pink may be fine for a few months but then you might welcome a season with softer colors in more conventional combinations.

ABOVE: Haphazard color mixtures can often be pleasing in a windowbox, as in this medley of red, blue, white and yellow.
OPPOSITE: Foliage color plays an important part in this restrained scheme in blue, white and pink.

Flowers are such successful self-publicists that it is easy to forget that plants are not solely dependent on them for color. It is rewarding to create gardens, even those as small as windowboxes, in which flowers play little or no part, and here it is the interplay of foliage that counts. The results can be wonderfully rich and subtle combinations of color, shape and texture.

It would, however, be a gardener of very severe mind who would willingly abandon completely the extraordinary range of colors that flowers provide. For the window gardener it is, after all, flowers that offer the greatest scope for decorative combinations, especially in terms of their relationship to buildings and to the world beyond the window. One of the successes of plant breeding is the dramatic extension of the range of flower color that it has made available to the gardener. All the rainbow hues of cultivated ornamentals are worth exploiting to the full, whether in harmonious or daring combinations.

Color Combinations

There are no simple rules for color coordination that easily explain why colors that might be expected to clash, so often happily combine. A few pointers can steer the way towards effective results, but the best lessons are learned by observing how other gardeners have married colors successfully.

It is flowers that dominate most color schemes, and combining them usually presents no problem at all. Close harmonies in yellows often uneasy with each other at close quarters, but many pink flowers have yellow centers that can usefully serve to marry the two colors together. The most difficult flowers to place are bright doubles with heavy heads, like some of the French and African marigolds (*Tagetes*), which can stand out as crude blobs of color, rather than blending into an appealing scheme. If they are used, they are best set against copious foliage.

and oranges or pinks and reds are often effective, as are bold contrasts, for example of purple and gold. What is more difficult is to give commonplace combinations distinction, but the addition of an unusual shade or hue can be enough to transform an ordinary window-box into an arresting display.

Many discordant combinations are eased by the fact that most flowers are not of a single color. A tinge at the edge, a contrasting eye or shading at the throat can provide a link between colors that clash. Pink and yellow are

LEFT: Pale colors can dominate by sheer mass even when there is competition from much stronger hues. Here the soft pink of pendulous begonias holds the eye in a rich planting that includes nemesias, lobelia, impatiens, petunias and Swan River daisy.

ABOVE: Many perennial pinks have prettily marked flowers. Here the dark striation intensifies the ground color and also the hint of mauve-pink in an ivy-leaved pelargonium.

OPPOSITE: Frilled white petunias add a cool finish to the bold contrast of pastel pink wall and dark windowbox and shutters.

The use of foliage, in fact, solves many of the problems presented by uncomfortable juxtapositions of flower color. It provides, too, countless color variations of its own, including a spectrum of greens ranging from near blue to pale lemon. Another delicate range is to be found in the greys, for example among the artemisias, helichrysums, sages and lavenders. Varying from silvery white at one extreme to slate blue at the other, greys are the most tactful of all intermediaries between aggressive colors.

Plenty of foliage plants, however, are much less reticent in their coloring. There are numerous variations on purple, bronze and red, the purple-leaved sage (*Salvia officinalis* 'Purpurascens') being among the quietest of them. Really startling is the near pure black of the grass-like *Ophiopogon planiscapus nigrescens*, especially when it is seen against the yellow foliage of the golden-leaved creeping jenny (*Lysimachia nummularia* 'Aurea'). Golds and yellows brighten many variegated plants, and splashing and edging of leaves, often in

attractively quirky forms, can also occur in creamy white. The variegated strawberry (*Fragaria vesca* 'Variegata') and the pick of the variegated mints, *Mentha suaveolens* 'Variegata', are lovely cool combinations of green and near white. It must be conceded, however, that variegations, so beautiful in detail, can create an agitated effect when overused.

Autumn is the season for the most dramatic changes of foliage color, and it is also the time for berries, which can be as important as flowers in adding touches of vivid color. The best of the berrying shrubs, such as the gaultherias and skimmias, will hold their berries throughout much of the winter. The dwarf maples (*Acer*) are unmatched for the brilliance of their autumn foliage. They are of course too spreading for a normal windowbox but make beautiful container-grown plants for a yard or patio. Dwarf conifers often change color in winter, the greenish yellow of summer turning deep gold while dark greens turn bronze or purple.

As with beds and borders in the open garden, a personal preference for a particular shade of flower or foliage is the basis on which many planting schemes are built up. Windowboxes, however, relate so closely to architecture that color details of a building are important references to bear in mind. The more conscious the gardener is of using plants to decorate a house, the more important the paintwork of walls, doors, windows and shutters becomes in providing contrasting or harmonious backgrounds. For those living in apartments the view from inside is more important than the dressed exterior of a building. For them the inspiration for a color scheme might come from interior furnishing.

OPPOSITE: *Wallflowers* (Cheiranthus cheiri) *have taken over from daffodils in this striking yellow scheme using a grand arrangement of tiered containers.*

LEFT: *Close color harmonies using one kind of plant can form the basis of an appealing scheme such as this, in which pale yellow and deep yellow mimulus contrast with a light filling of blue lobelia.*

BELOW: *The windowbox has been painted yellow to complement this sunny scheme, which includes specimens of arctotis, gazania and nasturtium.*

Hot and Cool Schemes

One of the great pleasures of window gardening is that color schemes are easily changed from year to year. A summer using hot colors of tropical intensity can be followed a year later with equally pleasing effect by cool combinations of subtler, paler shades. There are plenty of plants to choose from whichever you opt for, and some of the most popular container plants, pelargoniums and nasturtiums among them, have cultivars in both strong and pastel colors.

When vibrant reds and oranges are assembled in large masses in the open garden, the effect can be overpowering, but on the small scale of a window garden these hot colors usually seem bright and cheerful rather than garish. Even in dull weather they can conjure up ideas of Californian or Mediterranean sunshine. If they do seem too aggressive, it is usually because the flowers themselves are overbred, to the point of being coarse and blobby. It is almost always a good idea to use foliage generously when a scheme is dominated by hot colors. Nature organizes this well

BELOW: Impatiens in luminous pale colors or fiery shades are useful in windowboxes that are in part shade. In this windowbox, the vivid scarlet of the impatiens is slightly cooled by the blue of lobelia.

OPPOSITE: Planting with a mass of strongly colored flowers on this grandiose scale is not easy to pull off. The sheer vitality of the scheme goes a long way towards making it successful, but the control exerted by the architectural framework and the airiness of the planting also help to moderate the riotous effect of the color combination.

herself, giving the brash flower colors of rhododendrons, for example, a foil of dark green leaves, and there are plenty of suitable plants that you could use to achieve the same effect in a windowbox. *Skimmia* works well, also the dense greens of dwarf conifers, the fresh hues of some of the culinary herbs, and ferns and hostas. Grey can sometimes be a better choice than green, and *Helichrysum petiolare*, with its trailing stems, is an attractive alternative to the artemisias, which tend to be a good deal bushier in their habit.

The potential of hot colors is not limited to summer-flowering annuals. Seasonal displays can be created with bulbs in clashing, vibrant colors, or with the bright reds and oranges of winter berries.

Pale blues, creamy yellows, soft pinks and other pastel colors are less widely used as the key plants in window gardens than they deserve to be. The reason may be that the short-term plants offered by garden centers and nurseries are often available only in stronger colors, and that to get the pastel shades that you want means raising your own plants from seed.

Just as the value of rich, deep hues can be wasted if they are not shown off by pale flowers or light-colored foliage, pastel colors need an appropriate background. Setting them in front of a strong or deep color is an obvious solution. A window often appears as a dark recess and enhances pale colors to good effect. Deep green foliage helps too, providing a base over which pastel colors can float lightly. However, a delicate impression can be achieved by showing one pale color against another, pastel blue or white flowers, for instance, against a wall painted a soft pink.

OPPOSITE: Blue, grey and white make a classic cool combination. Here, a pale lavender petunia is married with a white browallia and the ever-useful, silver-grey of an artemisia.

RIGHT: The purples of nierembergias, Swan River daisy, verbenas and Scaevola aemula *enhance the cool silver of foliage plants that include* Santolina chamaecyparissus, Lamium maculatum *'White Nancy' and* Thymus × citriodorus *'Silver Queen'.*

BELOW: In some of the loveliest pansies luminous pale rims outline deep, velvety faces.

Colorful Tins and Pots

Brightly decorated improvised containers and painted pots can form the basis of an eye-catching display. Choose bold, simple plants that can hold their own visually.

WHAT YOU NEED:
A selection of decorated tins
A selection of terracotta pots
Hammer and large nail
Blue water-based paint
Brush
Crocks or other drainage material
1 gallon/4.5 litres of soilless potting compost

A selection of plants with red and orange flowers, including dahlias and verbenas

A selection of plants with yellow flowers, including French and African marigolds (*Tagetes*) and argyranthemums.

1. From a collection of tins, choose those you wish to preserve intact.
2. Use a hammer and nail to knock four or five drainage holes in selected tins.
3. Use tins without drainage holes as receptacles for plants in plastic pots. A polythene lining gives added protection.
4. Use a water-based paint to color terracotta pots to suit an overall color scheme.
5. Plant up the containers and arrange them on the sill or staging, according to colors.

SHAPE, TEXTURE AND FRAGRANCE *Making the most of plants*

Our appreciation of plants is very much dominated by our response to color. The eye is so delighted by the richness of the palette of flowering plants that their other qualities are often neglected. The scale of the open garden sometimes contributes to this bias, broad effects counting for more than detail. There is, however, a growing awareness among gardeners that color is not everything. There is a renewed interest in flowers with interesting forms and textures and an increasing reliance on foliage plants with leaves of an unusual texture, size or ornamental shape.

The limitations imposed by gardening in restricted spaces such as windowboxes and other containers are sometimes a source of frustration. The intimate scale of a window garden, however, does provide an opportunity to appreciate and exploit all the ornamental qualities that plants possess. More than that, schemes making the most of contrasts of shape, size and texture in foliage and flowers have the

ABOVE: Cherry pie (Heliotropium) nestles at the foot of the dainty Tweedia caerulea, a tender plant with seedpods that burst open to release a ball of fluff.
OPPOSITE: The small-leaved or Greek basil is a fine-textured and deliciously aromatic plant.

edge on those which concentrate exclusively on flower color. Variety in plant habit, the way plants carry themselves, is an important aspect of window gardening: while trailing plants are needed to break the hard edges of containers, they are often not substantial enough to form the main component of a planting scheme and need to be backed by plants of more erect or bushy habit.

A window garden is on such a small scale that it seems a lot to ask of it that it should appeal to the sense of smell as well as to the eye. It is a poor garden, though, that has no evocative scents or spicy aromas. Among the plants suitable for window gardens many are strongly scented or have aromatic foliage, and, although to choose them exclusively would prove unnecessarily limiting, the inclusion of one or two, at least during some periods of the year, contributes an added dimension to the window garden. Many are simply ornamental, but others are useful kitchen herbs as well as being attractive plants.

Shape and Form

A flick through an illustrated plant catalog reveals an extraordinary range of flower form and size. Daisy shapes predominate, neat and starry as in the Swan River daisy (*Brachyscome*), bold and gaudily handsome in gazanias. But there are also nodding bells and upturned cups, trumpets and funnels, flat faces and helmets, lipped and spurred flowers. Plants present their flowers in a variety of ways too. Aside from a simple flower per stem, there are open clusters, tight heads, spikes and sprays. Flowers can be upward-facing, outward-facing or elegantly drooping. This infinite variety is due in part to the diversity of nature but is also the result of centuries of selection and breeding. As well as increases in flower size and color range, doubling and other transformations have greatly enlarged the repertoire of flower forms available.

The range of leaf shape and size, impressively varied too, is less the result of selective breeding than of natural diversity. Botanists use an extensive vocabulary to describe the many variations, from the straps and spikes of grassy leaves, through simple circular and elliptical outlines to fingered and jagged shapes, fronds and compounds. The growth habit of plants also shows great diversity; some are light and airy, some dense and bushy, others narrow and upright, sprawling or mounded, weeping or trailing.

Even on the scale of a windowbox or a collection of large and small containers, a lot can be done to exploit the many possibilities that garden plants have to offer. By all means consider color combinations when bringing plants together, but it is also important to bear in mind contrasts of leaf shape and texture, flower size and form.

OPPOSITE: Balcony railings space out the long, trailing stems of Glechoma hederacea *'Variegata' and pink pelargoniums, which stand out boldly against the black-painted woodwork.*

RIGHT: The cacti include some of the most curious plant textures and shapes, and a collection of them can make a fascinating outdoor display in summer.

BELOW: A single specimen of a compact sedum combines interesting texture with a pleasing rounded shape in this small windowsill pot.

Texture

We often fail to recognize the part played by texture in our overall impression of a flower. The velvety finish of pansies and petunias, for example, intensifies the rich colors that are often found in these flowers. The fragile charm of poppies owes as much to the tissue-paper texture of their petals as to their simple shape and clear colors. The glistening sheen on the bright, narrow petals of mesembryanthemums contributes to their attention-seeking dazzle. Perhaps the most curious of all textures is the mealy powdering that in some auriculas (*Primula auricula*) seems to have spread from the leaf and stem to the flower surface.

The texture of flowers may be something to appreciate rather than deliberately to exploit

ABOVE: Contrasts of flower and leaf size, shape and texture enhance the visual appeal of this well-thought-out windowbox collection in pastel shades, the whole dominated by the soft, rounded leaves of a variegated pelargonium.

in planting schemes, but the potential of foliage, with its tactile and light-reflecting qualities, should be fully used. This is especially important in shade, where plants with glossy leaves, such as bergenias and skimmias, create a brighter impression than plants with mat leaves. Variegated ivies and euonymus demonstrate the extent to which a shiny surface enhances leaf color. The complex shadowing of ribbed, crinkled, quilted and corrugated leaves can become a dramatic element in a mixture of foliage and flowers. The leaves of hostas, aside from their remarkable range of color, are so varied in texture that contrasts can be made between smooth and shiny, ribbed and corrugated types.

There are many degrees of hairiness in leaves, producing very different effects. Coarse hairiness, as in *Tolmiea menziesii*, gives a rough finish, but a close, dense cover of small hairs can create a luxurious suede-like texture, as can be found in some of the scented-leaved pelargoniums. Softly hairy leaves, like for example those of lady's mantle (*Alchemilla mollis*), often trap water in beautiful quick-silver drops. A covering of fine hairs produces the silvery or white finish of grey-leaved plants. At one extreme these can be nearly woolly or densely felted, as in the boldly cut *Senecio bicolor cineraria* 'White Diamond'; at the other they can have the silkiness of the leaves of *Artemisia schmidtiana*.

A fine, hairy surface to a leaf is usually a way of reducing water loss. Fleshiness is another defense against drought, and the three-dimensional quality it gives to foliage can be very attractive in plants such as sedums. They sometimes complete their water conservation measures with a waxy coating, and this

glaucous finish can be effectively contrasted with stronger colors. In a collection of rock-garden plants the waxy *Sedum spathulifolium* 'Cape Blanco' is well set off by the rich colors in the leaf rosettes of sempervivums.

ABOVE: Of the pelargoniums, the Regals have the most elegantly shaped and color-saturated flowers. Here they are contrasted effectively with the large leaves and heavy, velvety flowers of a richly colored tuberous begonia.

Fragrant Flowers and Aromatic Foliage

Raising plants above ground level often leads to the discovery of scents that go undetected in the open garden. The fresh scents of many spring flowers — among them polyanthus and primroses as well as bulbs such as species crocuses, grape hyacinths (*Muscari*) and irises — are best appreciated close up. A few bulbs have perfumes that carry well, the classics being hyacinths and jonquils. The wallflower, which is at its peak in late spring, has not only delightfully velvety flowers but a soft, warm scent to match.

Good scented flowers for summer include several annuals, and of these the queen is the sweet pea, of which there are dwarf kinds short enough to be grown in windowboxes. Lilies are the outstanding summer bulbs and some have magnificent scents. Most are too tall-growing for windowboxes but, if you can, try stationing pots of one of the easiest, the regal lily (*Lilium regale*), beneath a window. In midsummer its purple-stained white trumpets, carried on stems about 5ft/1.5m high, broadcast an exotic, voluptuous scent that will pervade a room. The spicily scented pinks (*Dianthus*) are more easily managed in a windowbox or, better still, in pots.

A few well-scented plants have flowers of little ornamental value. The two most commonly grown are night-scented stock (*Matthiola incana*) and mignonette (*Reseda odorata*). A few specimens tucked into a display of container-grown plants will add their sweet scent to a collection of showy flowers.

Chief among the aromatic plants are the traditional culinary herbs such as sage, thyme and rosemary. Grow them for their usefulness but savor, too, the evocation of the sunny Mediterranean released by touching their leaves. They can be combined with flowering plants or included in an aromatic collection, as on pages 70–1. Outstanding among other aromatic plants are the scented-leaved pelargoniums. Light bruising releases powerful scents of rose, apple, orange, lemon, nutmeg and pine as well as less easily identified spicy and pungent aromas.

OPPOSITE: *This view from a window takes in a deliciously fragrant collection of scented and aromatic plants. Ornamentals include scented-leaved pelargoniums, santolina, tobacco plant (*Nicotiana*) and white-flowered pinks (*Dianthus*). Thyme, sage and rosemary are among the useful herbs.*

ABOVE: *The addition of a few fragrant flowers adds another dimension to a planting scheme in a windowbox. This display includes short-growing sweet peas and nasturtiums, both well scented.*

Foliage for Shade

Elegant fronds and clumps of large leaves brought together on a handsome stand make a superb foliage display under a shady window.

YOU WILL NEED:
Plant stand 33in/84cm in height, top section 30in/ 75cm × 10in/25cm
Selection of terracotta pots
1 gallon/5 litres soilless or, preferably, loam-based compost
Crocks or other material for good drainage
Slow-release fertilizer
Trowel

For top level:
1 *Fragaria vesca* 'Variegata'
1 *Hosta sieboldii*
1 *Hosta* × *tardiana* 'Halcyon'
1 ivy

1 *Polypodium vulgare* 'Cornubiense'
1 *Polystichum setiferum* 'Plumosum'
For bottom level:
1 *Asplenium scolopendrium*
1 *Athyrium niponicum pictum*
2 ivies
1 *Mitella caulescens*

1. Assemble materials.
2. Mix a slow-release fertilizer with the compost at the recommended rate.
3. Place a layer of old crocks in the base of pots before part-filling with compost.
4. Plant in individual pots, ensuring that the roots are not cramped. Top up with compost and firm before watering thoroughly. Arrange on the plant stand.

An Aromatic Collection

To enhance an aromatic collection add one or two plants with a long flowering season. The plants here like a free-draining compost.

YOU WILL NEED:
Wooden windowbox, about 3ft/90cm long, 9in/25cm wide and 8in/20cm deep
Black polythene sheet, approximately 4 × 2½ft/ 120 × 75cm (optional)
1 quart/1 litre coarse shingle
2 gallons/10 litres soilless potting compost
2lb/1kg silver sand
Trowel

1 common sage (*Salvia officinalis*)
1 purple-leaved sage (*S. o.* 'Purpurascens')
1 gold variegated sage (*S. o.* 'Icterina')

2 purple-flowered dwarf lavenders (*Lavandula × intermedia* 'Twickel Purple')
1 dwarf white lavender (*L. angustifolia* 'Nana alba')
1 pink-flowered hyssop (*Hyssopus officinalis roseus*)
2 double-flowered chamomiles (*Chamaemelum nobile* 'Flore Pleno')
4 scented-leaved pelargoniums
1 miniature regal pelargonium

1. Assemble the ingredients.
2. To make a free-draining mixture add silver sand to a standard compost (not more than 1 part sand to 9 parts compost by bulk).
3. If lining the windowbox with black polythene, first slash holes in the base for drainage. Put in a layer of coarse shingle to a depth of 1–2in/2.5–5cm before filling the box with compost.
4. Carefully knock the plants out of their pots and plant them into the compost.

PLANTS AND PRACTICALITIES

All the information you need to choose and grow beautiful windowbox plants

There is no shortage of plants suitable for the window garden, and any selection inevitably leaves out some that are excellent. In making this choice, my aim has been to include representatives of all the main categories of plants suitable for window gardens and to present a mixture of familiar and less well-known plants. My hope is that gardeners will take inspiration from what they see in the window gardens of others and will themselves derive pleasure from experimenting with a wide range of different plants.

The following symbols have been used throughout this section to indicate the growing conditions that best suit individual plants.

- ☼ Full sun
- ☼ Part shade
- ✺ Shade
- ▽ Free-draining compost
- ▼ Ordinary compost
- ▼ Moist compost

ABOVE: The deep burgundy, Regal pelargonium 'Lord Bute' looks dramatic in a terracotta pot painted blue and gold.
OPPOSITE: Common annuals, such as fuchsias, calceolarias and ivy-leaved pelargoniums, can create a bold, lively display.

HARDINESS

Reference in the following entries is sometimes made to a plant's hardiness, that is its ability to stand up to cold temperatures. Plants that are tender in inland areas or above sea level, failing to survive outdoors in winter, may well flourish outdoors all year in more favorable conditions, such as on or near the coast.

Many factors affect a plant's ability to resist low temperatures. Sudden drops in temperature are usually more damaging than a steady fall, and cold winds are more destructive than low temperatures in a sheltered position. Very young and old plants suffer more than those that are established and still in their prime, and wood that has been well ripened by plenty of summer sunshine stands up better than soft growth produced by excessive nitrogen or wet conditions. Container-grown plants are generally at greater risk of frost damage than those growing in the open garden.

ANNUALS, BIENNIALS AND BEDDING PLANTS

Annuals are plants that complete their life cycle within one growing season and can be disposed of once they have finished flowering. There are two distinct kinds of ornamental annual: hardy annuals, which in many parts of the temperate world survive frost and can be sown outdoors, and half-hardy annuals, which are vulnerable to frost. Biennials complete their life cycle in two years, germinating and producing leaves in the first year and flowering the year after. The plants listed here include true annuals and biennials and also several shrubs and perennials (plants that grow and flower season after season) that in temperate regions are usually grown as annuals. These can be loosely defined as bedding plants.

Many of the species described are easily raised from seed but are frequently bought as young plants in late spring, ready for moving into containers. A number of the tender perennials normally grown as annuals are not difficult to raise from cuttings, and overwintered specimens can provide material for new stocks.

Antirrhinum ☼ ▽

Some of the appeal of the snapdragon (*A. majus*), a perennial normally grown as an annual, is undoubtedly lost in the dwarf forms, but the short-growing cultivars do mean that a free-flowering plant with a wide range of colors can be grown in windowboxes. In the Tom Thumb strain, which is about 6in/15cm high, the flowers have the prominent tubular lip so characteristic of the species. There are also dwarf kinds with open-petalled flowers.

Arctotis ☼ ▽

The half-hardy perennial hybrids (*Arctotis × hybridum*) are often grown as half-hardy annuals. The daisy flowers, which are borne profusely throughout summer, come in a wide range of colors that includes orange, bronze and mahogany as well as pinks, reds and white, sometimes with handsomely marked dark centers. They are carried over grey foliage to make a plant with a height of about 1ft/30cm and a spread of 18in/45cm. The rich shades are useful in hot color schemes.

Bellis ☼ ◑ ▽

The giant, miniature button, and quilled forms of the perennial common daisy (*B. perennis*) are usually grown as biennials but some cultivars need to be propagated by division. These are excellent plants for spanning the gap between early bulbs and summer annuals. The flowers are pink and white and plants are rarely more than 6in/15cm high. Two old-fashioned miniature gems, about 4in/10cm in height, are the double pink 'Dresden China' and the double red 'Rob Roy'.

Brachyscome ☼ ▽

The Swan River daisy (*B. iberidifolia*) is a half-hardy annual up to 18in/45cm in height, covered with fragrant daisy flowers throughout summer. Colors include white, lavender, blue, pink and purple. Pinch out the tips of young plants to encourage bushiness.

Calendula ☼ ▽

The pot marigold (*C. officinalis*) produces a long succession of orange or yellow daisy flowers from late spring to autumn and is a cheerful companion for other warm-colored annuals. The Art Shades strain offers some subtle pastels. Regular deadheading and pinching back will keep plants below 2ft/60cm. Pot marigolds tolerate poor soils, but flower size improves and the proportion of doubles increases if the compost is of medium quality.

Cheiranthus ☼ ▽

The dwarf forms of the common wallflower planted up in autumn will give a mass of sweetly scented velvety flowers in mid- to late spring, coinciding with the main tulip season. The Tom Thumb strain grows to a height of about 10in/25cm. Wallflower colors range from pastel creams, yellows and pinks to rich reds, purples and mahogany. Unfortunately, it is difficult to buy seed of dwarf kinds in single colors. Pinching back young plants encourages bushy growth.

Convolvulus ☼ ▽

The shrubby *C. sabatius* (*C. mauritanicus*), often grown as an annual, gives a long succession of blue funnel-shaped flowers throughout summer. This is a sprawler, about 6in/15cm high but with a spread of 3ft/90cm or more, and it is superb in a tall pot on its own.

Dahlia ☼ ▼

Dwarf dahlias are half-hardy perennials, but plants raised from seed sown in heat during late winter and early spring will flower freely from midsummer until the first frosts and are useful to bring life to containers when other plants are beginning to look tired. Several seed strains are available, with double and semi-double flowers in a bright color range including yellows, oranges, reds and white. The Redskin strain, 18in/45cm high, has dark bronze foliage.

DIASCIA ☀ ▽

Most of the perennial diascias are not reliably hardy but give a long flowering season when grown as annuals. 'Ruby Field' is a sprawling plant up to 6in/15cm high, which is covered in summer with dusty pink flowers. *D. vigilis (D. elegans)* is slightly smaller, with bright green leaves and rich pink flowers. Trim off dead flowers regularly to maintain a continuous display.

ESCHSCHOLZIA ☀ ▽

Californian poppies are hardy annuals that carry masses of bright satiny flowers over ferny foliage in summer. Plants are normally under 16in/40cm and mixtures include shades of orange, yellow, pink and crimson. Single colors are also available. Eschscholzias are best for containers that can be moved on after the main bloom, although deadheading will prolong flowering.

FELICIA ☀ ▽

The blue marguerite (*Felicia amelloides*), a half-hardy perennial that is generally grown as an annual, needs sun to open its sky-blue daisies, which are borne profusely throughout summer. The flowers of 'Santa Anita', a cultivar that grows about 12in/30cm tall with a spread of 18in/45cm, are of particularly good size and color. Foliage and flowers go well together on the variegated blue

The New Guinea hybrids of Impatiens *provide extravagant foliage in a windowbox.*

marguerite, which makes a good addition to combinations of blues, creams and yellows.

GAZANIA ☀ ▽

The hybrid gazanias, tender perennials normally grown as annuals, have showy daisy flowers, predominantly in yellows and oranges, often rayed or with eye-catching markings around the disc. The flowers, which close at night, are produced in abundance over a long summer season. Deep green foliage with a felted white underside is a bonus. Plants are generally about 12in/30cm in height, with a spread of about 18in/45cm. They are a good choice for an exposed but sunny position.

IMPATIENS ☀ ☼ ▽

Few plants are so free-flowering in part shade as busy Lizzies. These perennials, usually grown as half-hardy annuals, are compact plants, about 8in/20cm in height, with flowers of dazzling luminosity in white or shades of red, pink and orange. The New Guinea Hybrids, such as the F_1 'Tango', have good bronzy foliage.

LOBELIA ☀ ☼ ▽

The bedding plant *L. erinus*, a half-hardy perennial grown as an annual, is almost too familiar as a component of windowboxes and other containers. It does not, however, do to be snobbish about a plant that bears masses of small flowers without interruption from late spring until autumn in a color range that includes violet, many shades of blue, purple, pink and white, and which offers a choice between cascading and compact bushy cultivars. Its virtues include being easily pleased.

MIMULUS ☼ ✳ ▼
The monkey flowers, of which good F_1 hybrids are available, are usually grown as half-hardy annuals. The velvety snapdragon flowers, in gold, orange and red, often beautifully shaded, blotched and speckled, are carried from early summer to autumn. The Malibu F_1 hybrids offer a good color range, the trailing plants growing to 10in/25cm.

NICOTIANA ✳ ▽
Tobacco plants are half-hardy perennials that are usually grown as half-hardy annuals. The dwarf F_1 hybrids are faintly-scented, free-flowering plants about 1ft/30cm in height with a color range that includes white, pinks, purples, reds and a cool lime green. They like rich living, and look well fronted by trailing plants.

OSTEOSPERMUM ☼ ▽
The African daisies (sometimes listed as *Dimorphotheca*) are tender perennials commonly grown as annuals. They produce masses of cheerful flowers over a long summer season. The most useful for containers are under 1ft/30cm high and have trailing stems. On *O. ecklonis prostratum* the white petals and blue disc make a distinguished combination. Good purples include 'African Queen' and 'Hampton Court Purple'. 'Cannington John', with spoon-shaped petals, and 'Langtrees' are desirable pinks. Plants begin flowering when young and it is

generally possible to make a good selection from unnamed plants.

PELARGONIUM ✳ ▽
Pelargoniums, misleadingly known as geraniums, are mainstays of container gardening, flowering over a long period in sunny positions and tolerating fairly dry conditions. Although frequently treated as annuals, pelargoniums are tender evergreen shrubs that can be overwintered and easily propagated from cuttings.

Zonal pelargoniums have rounded leaves, often boldly zoned or marked, and dense rounded flowerheads carried in prolific succession into autumn. The flowers may be single, semi-double or double. Of the many cultivars available in a wide color range, the compact kinds, 8–20in/20–50cm high, are best suited to windowboxes. Good representatives include: 'Fantasie' – double white; 'Friesdorf' – single red with dark foliage; 'Little Alice' – double orange with dark leaves. Seed of F_1 hybrids is readily available, and plants that flower in summer can be raised from sowings in heat during winter.

Ivy-leaved pelargoniums, which form cascades of shiny fleshy leaves on stems that may be 3ft/90cm or more in length, also have a long flowering season. There is a good range of colors in single, semi-double or double flowers. 'L'Elegante' is a strikingly variegated example, with foliage as ornamental as the pale mauve flowers.

Regal pelargoniums live up to their name with large, splendid, often frilled flowers in a wide color range, in many cases with wonderfully rich markings

and shading. They have, however, a shorter flowering season than Zonal or Ivy-leaved pelargoniums. Be on the look-out for compact named cultivars, such as 'Hazel', with violet-purple flowers, or 'Pompeii', with a pink-tinged edge to nearly black petals.

Although their flowers are less showy than those of other pelargoniums, the scented-leaved kinds have delicious scents of nutmeg, oranges, roses and other fragrances.

PETUNIA ☼ ✳ ▽
The free-flowering hybrid petunias, perennials that are almost invariably grown as half-hardy annuals, are commonplace container plants and yet difficult to beat if the aim is a long-lasting, colorful display. A distinction is normally made between Multifloras, with small flowers, Grandifloras, with large, often frilled, flowers, and the intermediate Floribundas. There are numerous F_1 hybrids, singles and doubles, and a color range that includes white, pinks, blues, purples and yellows, among which there are picotees and bold bicolors. Choose weather-resistant cultivars for windowboxes in exposed positions. Excessive feeding will produce leaf at the expense of flowers.

PRIMULA ☼ ✳ ▼
The polyanthus is a hybrid primrose, about 6in/15cm in height, that is usually grown as a biennial. Most of the modern strains produce heads of large flowers in vivid colors, including reds, yellows, blues, pinks and white. They give a long display, starting in winter. There are

many choice forms of *P. vulgaris*, including gold-laced and double kinds, that are just as useful in containers.

SENECIO ☼ ⊽

Some of the slightly tender shrubby senecios that have good grey foliage are generally grown as annuals. These include *S. bicolor cineraria* 'White Diamond' (*S. maritima* 'White Diamond'), which has beautifully cut and felted leaves. It makes a bushy plant to 2ft/60cm and is ideal for calming bright flower colors.

TAGETES ☼ ⊽

The African and French marigolds (*T. erecta* and *T. patula*) and the crosses between them are half-hardy annuals producing masses of rather congested flowers in shades of yellow and orange, sometimes with rich mahogany markings. There are several dwarf strains under 12in/30cm in height. All flower through summer into autumn. A much lighter effect is achieved with cultivars of *T. tenuifolia pumila*. 'Lemon Gem' and 'Golden Gem', for example, are bushy plants about 8in/20cm high that produce a profusion of single flowers over finely cut leaves.

TROPAEOLUM ☼ ⊽

Nasturtiums (*T. majus*) are cheerful and easy hardy annuals, bearing numerous spurred flowers over a long summer season if planted in sun and regularly deadheaded. Colors include orange, pink and red, and various shades of pale or dark yellow. The attractive rounded leaves may need spraying to control

aphids. The compact cultivars are rarely more than 12in/30cm high but some are more trailing than others. The Dwarf Jewel Mixture and Whirlybird strains have semi-double flowers, and those of the latter are upward facing. 'Empress of India' is a good cultivar, with splendid deep crimson flowers.

VERBENA ☼ ⊽

The hybrid verbenas, perennials that are usually grown as half-hardy annuals, carry tight clusters of flowers through summer into autumn. Upright kinds are normally less than 18in/45cm in height and many are lower, with a spread of 2–3ft/60–90cm. The sprawlers, generally smaller-flowered than the other kinds, are good at insinuating themselves

Violas are a charming, long-flowering choice for a small-scale windowsill display.

among other plants to give touches of purple, mauve, pink, red and white. To prolong flowering, deadhead regularly and feed at the recommended intervals with a liquid fertilizer.

VIOLA ☼ ✿ ⊽

The popular bedding pansies and violas, hybrids of perennial species, are usually grown as biennials or annuals. Plants are rarely more than 6in/15cm high but there are considerable differences in flower size. The velvety flowers of pansies can be as much as 4in/10cm across and the overall outline is rounded. Viola flowers are smaller and, in the definition of the petals, closer in character to those of the species. There is a good range of single colors from black, deep purples and chestnut to white and pale pastels. There are also charming combinations of colors – some with gentle shadings, others with more striking contrasts – often consisting of a dark mask superimposed on lighter colors.

The flowering season can last for several months between spring and autumn and is prolonged by regular deadheading and feeding. The winter-flowering pansies, such as the Universal F_1 hybrids, are particularly valuable in making a cheerful display out of the main flowering season. The violas are excellent fillers to combine with other summer-flowering plants. Good examples, some of which need to be propagated vegetatively, include: 'Irish Molly' – greenish gold; 'Jackanapes' – deep rust and yellow; 'Molly Sanderson' – black with yellow eye; 'Prince Henry' – violet-purple with yellow throat.

BULBS

This term is used broadly to cover plants with underground storage organs. While those of daffodils are true bulbs, containing the new plant in embryo, those of crocuses, for example, are strictly speaking corms, consisting of a globular food reservoir at the base of the stem. Most bulbs and corms are sold dry in late summer or early autumn, and should be planted promptly.

BEGONIA ☼ ✿ ▼
The hybrid tuberous begonias are showy plants with large, rose-like, double flowers that are borne freely throughout summer. The colors include white and many shades of red, pink, yellow and orange. The Pendula hybrids are more slender plants with hanging stems and smaller flowers. This group is used mainly in hanging baskets but a single specimen can look attractive in a tall pot. Start begonia tubers into growth under glass in early spring and move plants outdoors in early summer. Choose a sheltered place as stems are easily damaged by wind.

CROCUS ☼ ▽
Most of the species crocuses have a relatively short but splendid season in late winter or early spring. The flowers, often subtly shaded or attractively marked, open in full sun and many have a honey scent. They can be grown with other plants in windowboxes but are ideal for growing in shallow pots that can be moved on from a windowsill when the flowers begin to fade.

Among the best of those that flower in late winter or early spring are the cultivars of C. chrysanthus. All the following are about 3in/7.5cm in height: 'Advance' – yellow and bronze with exterior mauve shading; 'Cream Beauty' – pale yellow; 'Gipsy Girl' – yellow with purple feathering; 'Ladykiller' – purplish blue with white margin; 'Snowbunting' – white with faint purple feathering.

Other species of similar size that flower at the same time include the brilliant orange C. ancyrensis ('Golden Bunch') and the dark mauve C. sieberi 'Violet Queen'.

The large-flowered Dutch crocuses (C. vernus) are less refined than the species but make a bold effect planted in pots or windowboxes with other bulbs. Most grow 4–6in/10–15cm tall and flower in mid-spring, a few slightly earlier. The following are popular and reliable examples: 'Jeanne d'Arc' – white; 'Purpureus Grandiflorus' – purplish blue; 'Yellow Mammoth' – butter yellow; 'Vanguard' – early, with silvery purple outer petals and pale violet inner petals.

CYCLAMEN ☼ ✿ ✸ ▽
Two hardy dwarf species are choice autumn- and winter-flowering plants suitable for growing in pots on a shady sill. Their flowering season lasts for several weeks and their foliage, silver and beautifully marked, remains attractive for months, until the dormant season begins in early summer. The best known is C. hederifolium (C. neapolitanum), usually not more than 4in/10cm high, with pink or white flowers in early to mid-autumn. C. coum, a slightly smaller plant, bears magenta, pink or white flowers between early

winter and early spring. The leaves of the Pewter Group are almost completely silver. The corms of these two species should be covered by about 1in/2.5cm of compost.

In mild areas the tender C. persicum, familiar as an indoor plant, can be used in bold winter plantings of windowboxes, but these cyclamen will not continue to flower for long at temperatures below 55°F/13°C.

GALANTHUS ☼ ✿ ▽
Snowdrops have a relatively short season but they are among the advance guard of spring and are valuable for that. As with dwarf irises and species crocuses, both of which are good associates for them, pot-grown plants can be moved on as the flowers die. There are many cultivars and hybrids of the common snowdrop (G. nivalis), most under 8in/20cm. Their differences are best appreciated when seen close to. A starter's selection could include: 'Flore Pleno' – double; 'S. Arnott' – well shaped and scented; 'Viridapicis' – green spot on outer as well as inner petals. The vigorous hybrid G. × atkinsii has particularly large flowers. A more heavily-built snowdrop, G. elwesii, up to 10in/25cm tall, has grey-green leaves and green marks at both the base and apex of the inner segments. Snowdrops can be planted as dry bulbs or 'in the green', that is to say in leaf, immediately after flowering.

HYACINTHUS ☼ ▼
The Dutch hyacinths, developed from H. orientalis, are among the most colorful and richly scented of bulbs that

flower in mid- to late spring. They are militarily erect to a height of 6–9in/15–22.5cm and tailor-made for pots or windowboxes that get full sun. Combining them in a windowbox with winter-flowering pansies, daisies (*Bellis perennis*) or the like helps to hide their stiffness. The following is a selection of the many named cultivars: 'Carnegie' – early, white; 'City of Haarlem' – late, pale yellow; 'Hollyhock' – early, double, carmine; 'Ostara' – early, deep blue; 'Pink Pearl' – early, pink.

Iris

Several dwarf bulbous irises are among the loveliest of early bulbs, standing up well to rough winter conditions. Many are strongly scented. They can be combined with semi-permanent rock-garden plants, grown on their own or mixed with other seasonal flowers. Among the best are *I. reticulata* and its numerous cultivars. These grow to about 6in/15cm and the flowers, predominantly in shades of blue and often with orange on the falls, survive snow and frost in late winter or early spring. All the following cultivars flower freely: 'Cantab' – pale blue; 'Clairette' – pale blue standards, deep blue falls; 'J.S. Dijt' – purplish red.

More heavily-built early dwarf irises include *I. danfordiae*. The dumpy flowers, about 4in/10cm high, are yellow spotted with green. It is difficult to keep plants going from year to year as after flowering the bulb tends to break up into many small bulblets. *I. histrioides* 'Major' is also a stocky plant, 4–6in/10–15cm in height, with a vivid orange crest against intense blue.

Lilium

Many lilies do well in containers but most are too tall for windowboxes. It is, however, worth looking out for short-growing new introductions that are suitable for being pot-grown on a sill. All the following hybrids are of manageable size and have the advantage of having upward-facing flowers: 'Elvin's Son' – 12in/30cm, late summer, yellow; 'Harvest' – 16in/40cm, midsummer, pale orange; 'Red Carpet' – 16in/40cm, midsummer, deep brick red.

It is important to plant bulbs as soon as they become available, preferably in autumn, say three to a pot.

For a dense display of spring crocuses and irises plant closely and in layers.

Muscari

The dense spikes of grape hyacinths, normally blue but also white, go well with other spring bulbs and flowers such as daisies (*Bellis perennis*) and polyanthus. Most are sweetly scented.

M. armeniacum is easy to grow, with spikes of vivid blue flowers about 6in/15cm tall in mid- to late spring. There is a double of this, 'New Creation', with flowers that fade through green and purple over a long season. The choicest of the whites is *M. botryoides album*, a neat albino form with flowers about 4in/10cm tall in mid-spring. The feathered hyacinth (*M. comosum* 'Plumosum') is a curiosity: its long-lasting flowers, which appear in late spring, are about 1ft/30cm tall and consist of feathery mauve filaments.

Narcissus ☼ ◉ ▯

The dwarf daffodils and jonquils are refined flowers that are ideal for windowboxes and pots, grown on their own or mixed with other spring flowers or foliage plants such as ivy. The leaves die down rather untidily, so, if grown among long-term plants, the bulbs need to be lifted once flowering is over.

The following selection is a small sample of those offered. In late winter or early spring there is 'Tête-à-Tête', 6–8in/15–20cm, generally with two or more short trumpets of deep yellow per stem. 'February Gold', 10in/25cm, is also early, with swept-back yellow petals and a deep yellow trumpet. 'Jack Snipe', slightly smaller than 'February Gold', has creamy swept-back petals and a short trumpet in pale yellow, and it will run on into mid-spring.

None of the following grows more than 8in/20cm high and all flower between mid- and late spring. 'Baby Moon' is a sweetly scented jonquil with many soft yellow flowers per stem. 'Hawera' and 'Petrel' are out of the same mold, with several elegant small-cupped flowers per stem. Those of 'Hawera' are yellow while those of 'Petrel' are white. 'Minnow' is similar in form, the flowers a refined shade of lemon yellow. 'Topolino' is a scaled-down trumpet daffodil, the trumpet yellow and the paler petals stylishly

twisted. 'Rip van Winkle' might be included as a curiosity for its bright yellow double flowers.

Among the last to flower is 'Silver Chimes', 12in/30cm high, with six small-cupped white flowers per stem.

Puschkinia ☼ ▯

The striped squill (*P. scilloides*, also listed as *P. libanotica*) makes an attractive pale addition to pots of early bulbs. In early spring stems up to 6in/15cm high carry as many as twenty light blue flowers, each segment with a darker central stripe.

Rhodohypoxis ☼ ▯

Although tiny, these are colorful plants that flower from spring to autumn. They are best grown in lime-free soil in shallow pots. *R. baurii* is the parent of most of the named cultivars, which are generally less than 3in/7.5cm in height. The petals overlap so that the flower seems to have no center. The color range includes white and various shades of pink and carmine. Protect corms from excessive dampness in winter by covering pots with glass.

Scilla ☼ ▯

The blue of *S. siberica* counts as one of the great delights of the first half of spring. The plant produces two or three stems per bulb, each one up to 6in/15cm high and carrying several bell-shaped flowers of intense blue. *S. mischtschenkoana* (*S. tubergeniana*) flowers a few weeks earlier. Its flower stems are shorter and the flowers themselves are paler in color, although attractively marked with a dark stripe.

Scillas are easy to grow and mix well with other spring-flowering bulbs or plants, such as violas and primroses.

Tulipa ☼ ▯

Among the many brilliantly colored tulips, there is a good choice of short-growing kinds that are suitable for pots and windowboxes. A succession of pot-grown tulips can provide a colorful display for almost three months of the year. In windowboxes a less formal effect can be created by combining them with foliage plants or winter pansies, polyanthus and other similarly early flowers. Among the pick are hybrids, mainly derived from short-growing species, particularly *T. fosteriana*, *T. greigii* and *T. kaufmanniana*. These include: 'Carlton' – 10in/25cm, mid-spring, double scarlet; 'Heart's Delight' – 10in/25cm, early spring, carmine exterior, white interior, leaves mottled; 'Johann Strauss' – 8–10in/20–25cm, early spring, exterior red edged with cream, interior white, mottled leaves; 'Red Riding Hood' – 8in/20cm, late spring, scarlet with black center, mottled leaves; 'Schonoord' – 12in/30cm, mid-spring, double white.

Among the mid-spring species, one of the most elegant is the slender *T. clusiana*, about 1ft/30cm high, with white flowers stained dark pink on the outside. Flowering at the same time is *T. praestans* 'Fusilier', with a stem 12in/30cm tall carrying three to five vivid scarlet flowers. A miniature for late spring is *T. linifolia* 'Bright Gem' (*T. batalinii* 'Bright Gem'), with yellow flowers stained orange, which is generally less than 6in/15cm tall.

HERBACEOUS PERENNIALS

Herbaceous perennials are plants that have no woody framework but re-grow every year and survive for an indefinite period. A few are evergreen but most are deciduous. Some culinary herbs (the mints, for example) are herbaceous perennials. The hardy perennials are major components of schemes in the open garden and can be used to great effect in windowboxes too. Rock-garden plants and alpines include small perennials as well as dwarf shrubs. The perennials described here, which include a few ferns and grasses, are hardy in many parts of the temperate world. Less hardy kinds that are often grown as annuals are described in Annuals, Biennials and Bedding Plants.

ADIANTUM ☼ ◑ ▉

The elegant maidenhair ferns include two hardy species suitable for shade. Their lightness is useful to offset stronger leaf shapes. The deciduous *A. pedatum*, 6–18in/15–45cm tall, has drooping fronds on purple stalks. *A. venustum*, 6in/15cm tall, has dark-stemmed fronds that turn brown in winter but are retained until the new fronds emerge, pink at first and then light green.

ALCHEMILLA ☼ ◑ ▉

An established plant of lady's mantle (*A. mollis*), 12–18in/30–45cm, is lovely for its soft fan-shaped leaves, holding glistening droplets of water, and for its sprays of yellow-green flowers in summer. Easier to accommodate are two charmers: *A. erythropoda*, 6in/15cm, is like a compact *A. mollis*, with starry lime-green flowers in midsummer; and

A. conjuncta, 4in/10cm, which has a silver backing to the leaves that shows on the cut edge. All are deciduous.

ANTHEMIS ☼ ▉

The white daisy flowers of *A. punctata cupaniana* are borne throughout summer on stems about 16in/40cm tall over a sprawling mat of silvery, finely cut leaves that are pleasantly aromatic. This makes a good main plant in a collection of alpines.

AQUILEGIA ☼ ◑ ▉

The dwarf columbines are good perennials to use with other rock-garden plants. They are grown principally for their spurred flowers, which are produced mainly in shades of violet, blue or purple, in late spring or early summer, but the leaves are beautifully divided and usually blue- or grey-green. *A. alpina* grows to about 12in/30cm, *A. bertolonii* to 6in/15cm and *A. flabellata* to about 8in/20cm.

ARMERIA ☼ ▉

The thrifts are compact, grassy evergreens bearing tight heads of long-lasting flowers. They are good for the corners or edges of troughs containing other rock-garden plants. The best-known kind is *A. maritima*, 6–12in/15–30cm in height and with a spread of 12in/30cm or more. Tight heads of pink flowers are carried from late spring to midsummer. Good named cultivars include: 'Alba' – white; 'Düsseldorfer Stolz' – wine red; 'Vindictive' – rose red. *A. juniperifolia* (*A. caespitosa*) makes a smaller tuft, up to 3in/7.5cm high, with pink flowers in late spring.

ARTEMISIA ☼ ▉

There are many excellent grey-leaved artemisias. *A. schmidtiana* has finely cut silver foliage of wonderful silkiness, and makes a little cushion about 4in/10cm high to combine with other lovers of sun and free drainage.

BERGENIA ☼ ◑ ● ▉

Bergenias have evergreen leaves, often red on the reverse that, in a sunny position, turn bronze or liverish in winter. The flowers, mainly pink but sometimes white, appear in spring. The smaller species and hybrids are suitable for a mixed long-term planting scheme: *B. stracheyi*, 6–8in/15–20cm, has rounded leaves and pink flowers; *B. s.* 'Alba' has white flowers. Hybrids include 'Admiral' and 'Wintermärchen'.

The grey foliage of Artemisia *makes a good contrast to purple petunias and lobelia.*

A box planted in gradations of purple contrasts the cushiony mass of Campanula *with the gaunt foliage of* Tradescantia.

CAMPANULA ☼ ▭

The smaller bellflowers are good companions for other sun-loving rock-garden plants and, usefully, flower later than most. *C. carpatica*, 8–12in/20–30cm, is the pick of them, with named forms giving a color range from deep violet through shades of blue to white. *C. garganica* and 'Birch Hybrid' are more compact. *C. portenschlagiana* and *C. poscharskyana* could take over a windowbox (*C. poscharskyana* 'Stella' is better behaved) but flower prolifically in almost any situation.

DIANTHUS ☼ ▭

The dwarf perennial pinks make tight cushions of narrow blue-grey leaves smothered in summer by prettily cut, often richly scented flowers, mainly in white or shades of pink and red. Even in flower they are usually less than 4in/10cm in height and make excellent miniature additions to a collection of rock-garden plants. Good examples include: 'Little Jock' – semi-double, pink with a dark eye; 'Pike's Pink' – semi-double, pink; 'Whatfield Gem' – double maroon with a pink fleck.

The two groups of hybrids known as Old-fashioned and Modern pinks are larger plants, the flower stems generally 12–16in/30–40cm in length. The Old-fashioned forms flower in early summer, but the Moderns have a longer season and often repeat in autumn. Both groups can be used in windowboxes but are better in simple pots, to be moved on when flowering has finished. 'Dad's Favorite', which is white with purple lacing, and the richly scented 'Mrs Sinkins', with an untidy white flower, belong to the Old-fashioned group. 'Prudence', which has crimson lacing on pale pink, and the strongly scented salmon pink 'Doris' are Moderns.

FESTUCA ☼ ▭

Several of the fescues are compact, tufty grasses under 12in/30cm in height and of a good grey-blue. Among the best colored are *F. amethystina*, *F. glauca* 'Blaufuchs' and *F. valesiaca glaucantha* 'Silbersee' (*F. glauca* 'Silver Sea').

FRAGARIA ☼ ◉ ▼

'Pink Panda' is an ornamental strawberry with bright green leaves and yellow-centered pink flowers, which appear over a long summer season. The appeal of the variegated wild strawberry (*F. vesca* 'Variegata') lies in the cool white and green of its leaves. Both plants are about 6in/15cm high and combine well with bold foliage plants.

HEUCHERA ☼ ◉ ▭

For year-round rich purple foliage few plants can beat *H. micrantha* 'Palace Purple'. In early summer the mound of palmate leaves, up to 2ft/60cm high, is topped by sprays of small white flowers. This is an excellent perennial for a long-term planting scheme with shrubs.

HOSTA ☼ ◉ ▼

Hostas are deciduous foliage plants of great distinction, with a wide color range, including blues and many variegations, and considerable differences in texture. Their trumpet flowers, mostly produced in midsummer, have a quiet beauty. Hostas come into leaf late but the smaller kinds are a useful addition to plantings in light shade. Among the best blues is *H. × tardiana* 'Blue Moon', with rounded leaves up to 8in/20cm long and grey-blue flowers. 'Vera Verde', with pale purple flowers and a white edge to lance-shaped green leaves, is of the same size. Two slightly larger variegated kinds are 'Ground Master', with purple flowers and a creamy, undulating edge to a green leaf, and *H. sieboldii kabitan*, with mauve flowers and a yellow leaf edged with green.

HOUTTUYNIA

A dazzling and unusual variegation is found in *H. cordata* 'Chameleon'. This is a sprawling deciduous plant, spreading from underground shoots, and is rarely more than 6in/15cm in height. Flashes of red, bronze and yellow show among the green of the well-shaped leaves. It is best in a pot on its own.

LAMIUM

Although rarely more than 6in/15cm in height, the dead nettles sprawl exuberantly, those with silver foliage making beautiful fillers in windowbox plantings. The hooded flowers of the following, though of secondary importance to the leaves, are a pretty addition in early summer: *L. galeobdolon* 'Herman's Pride' and *L. g.* 'Silberteppich' ('Silver Carpet') – silver and green leaves and yellow flowers; *L. maculatum* 'Beacon Silver' – silvery white leaves with pink flowers; *L. m.* 'White Nancy' – silver leaves and white

flowers. These plants will succeed reliably in almost any situation.

OPHIOPOGON

The black, strap-shaped leaves of *O. planiscarpus nigrescens*, which are carried all year round, can be used to make a bold contrast with bulbs, other short-growing perennials or bedding plants. The leaf clumps, about 10in/25cm high, spread slowly. The small, bell-shaped mauve flowers, which are borne in summer, are followed by long-lasting black berries.

PAPAVER

The alpine poppies, like small versions of the Iceland poppy, with cupped, tissue-paper flowers in summer, are rarely more than 8in/20cm in height and often much shorter. The flowers of *P. alpinum* can be white, yellow or red while those of *P. miyabeanum* are yellow. These are short-lived perennials that may be grown as annuals. They are most effectively combined with other rock-garden plants.

PHYLLITIS

The hart's tongue fern (*P. scolopendrium*, also listed as *Asplenium scolopendrium*) makes a large shuttlecock of evergreen strap-shaped leaves. Though their edges undulate beautifully, the leaves are not divided like a typical frond. This is an excellent foliage plant to grow in a shady container or windowbox.

SAXIFRAGA

The saxifrages include some choice alpines that could easily be grown in a sunny windowbox with a free-draining

compost. The mossy saxifrages, however, are lovely plants for light shade. The dense hummocks of foliage, when topped by a mass of starry flowers in the second half of spring, are about 10in/25cm high. 'Pearly King' is a good white and 'Triumph' is blood red.

SEDUM

Several dwarf stonecrops go well with sempervivums and other lovers of sun and free-draining soil. *S. spathulifolium* makes low hummocks, about 4in/10cm high, of tightly packed succulent leaves. In the cultivar 'Cape Blanco' these leaves are grey-white, and in 'Purpureum' a rich plum purple.

SEMPERVIVUM

The houseleeks have tight rosettes of fleshy leaves, generally less than 2in/5cm high, but these spawn more rosettes to form clusters as much as 12in/30cm across. Those of *S. arachnoideum*, the cobweb houseleek, are woven together with a web of hairs; this species also has attractive red flowers in early to midsummer. Many of the sempervivums offered are hybrids, with rosettes in subtle variations of pewter, plum and mahogany, and are best bought according to personal taste.

TOLMIEA

The maple-like leaves of the evergreen *T. menziesii* have the curious habit of spawning young plants. In 'Taff's Gold' some of the leaves are almost golden while others are finely speckled with gold. This is an excellent foliage plant to brighten a shaded windowsill and makes a good clump 1ft/30cm high.

SHRUBS

Shrubs, like trees, have a framework of woody stems. There is great diversity in their growth habit: some are ground-hugging miniatures for the rock garden; other are climbers, with long, lax stems, specially adapted to attach themselves to supports. The smaller shrubs are usually sold as container-grown specimens. The following selection includes a few dwarf conifers as well as deciduous and evergreen shrubs, all of which would be prime choices for a windowbox.

Argyranthemum

The tender perennial Paris daisies or marguerites (sometimes listed as *Chrysanthemum frutescens*) will flower throughout much of the year in warm climates. In cool areas they can be overwintered under glass or simply treated as annuals. Recent breeding has increased the color range and produced some excellent compact plants, although pinching out growth helps to keep all varieties neat and bushy. Two doubles that grow to about 18in/45cm are the white 'Snowflake' and the deep pink 'Vancouver'. 'Penny' is a compact pale yellow single.

Buxus

Few plants respond better to shaping than the common box (*B. sempervirens*). This small-leaved evergreen requires early formative pruning, but established specimens need only one trim a year, in late summer or early autumn. Simple geometric shapes add a formal note to windowboxes planted with seasonal flowers or long-term foliage, but box can also be treated more fancifully.

The austere shapes of clipped box make a formal statement for a town house.

Calluna

Heather or ling (*C. vulgaris*) is a small evergreen shrub normally 12–18in/30-45cm in height carrying spikes of clustered small flowers for several months, between midsummer and late autumn. There are numerous cultivars, some with double flowers, in a color range that includes white, pinks and purples. Variations in foliage color (not always marrying well with flower color) make these useful in long-term schemes with rock garden plants, or among shrubs such as dwarf conifers or other plants needing lime-free soil, like rhododendrons. The following are pointers to the flower and foliage color available: 'Allegro' – deep red flowers; 'Beoley Gold' – year-round golden foliage, white flowers; 'Darkness' – foliage deep green, flowers crimson; 'Robert Chapman' – foliage with gold, bronze and red tints, flowers purple; 'Silver Knight' – woolly silver foliage, pink flowers; 'Winter Chocolate' – foliage changing from yellow-green in spring, through red to winter bronze, flowers pale lavender.

Chamaecyparis

The evergreen conifer *C. lawsoniana* has given rise to numerous dwarf cultivars. These can give weight to a collection of rock-garden plants or small shrubs. The bright foliage of 'Green Globe', 1ft/30cm high, is good all year. For dense all-year gold one of the best is 'Minima Aurea', which slowly grows to a height of about 2ft/60cm.

ERICA ☼ ▟

There are several species of heath that are low evergreen shrubs carrying spikes of densely clustered flowers over long periods. Particularly useful for windowboxes are the winter-flowering kinds, mainly cultivars of *E. carnea*, most of which are about 10in/25cm in height. 'King George' is a compact free-flowering rosy pink example. Some have brightly colored foliage; 'Ann Sparkes', for instance, has a bronze tip to orange-yellow leaves.

All the cultivars of *E. carnea* will tolerate lime but those of the summer-flowering *E. cinerea* will not. Most of these are under 1ft/30cm in height and spread, and the color range includes pink, red, maroon and dark purple. Two splendid examples are 'Foxhollow Mahogany', with deep green leaves and mahogany red flowers, and 'Velvet Night', with purple-black flowers.

An annual trim will help to keep these plants compact.

EUONYMUS ☼ ◐ ▟

Among the best of the variegated evergreen shrubs for containers are cultivars of *E. fortunei* var. *radicans*. Their spread may be up to twice their height but excessive growth can be checked by trimming in spring. 'Emerald Gaiety', which forms a hummock about 2ft/60cm in height, has silvery variegation while 'Emerald 'n' Gold', about 18in/45cm high, has gold variegation that turns bronze-pink in winter. 'Sunspot', also about 18in/45cm high, has a central gold splash on dark green. These undemanding shrubs make a good base for a permanent scheme.

FUCHSIA ☼ ◐ ▟

Fuchsias bear troupes of balletic flowers, mainly in purples, pinks and white, over a long season in summer and autumn. These mainly tender shrubs are often replaced annually but may be overwintered under glass and are easily raised from cuttings. There are constant additions to the hundreds of hybrids, which include bushy kinds that grow to a height of 18in/45cm or less. 'Lady Thumb', red with a white skirt, and 'Tom Thumb', red with a mauve skirt, are good examples of compact hybrids. Predictable but attractive combinations may be made with blue flowers and silvery foliage.

GAULTHERIA ◐ ▟

Gaultherias and pernettyas (often still treated as botanically distinct) are evergreens with dark, glossy green leaves. The flowers, generally urn-shaped and white, sometimes tinged pink, are less important ornamentally than the showy berries, which last through winter. The most commonly grown are cultivars of *G. mucronata* (*Pernettya mucronata*), which make thick growth to about 2ft/60cm. The female fruiting cultivars need a male plant of *G. mucronata* to produce berries, which can be crimson ('Crimsoniana'), pale pink ('Parelmoer', also known as 'Mother of Pearl') or white ('Sneeuwwitje', also known as 'Snow White'). 'Bell's Seedling', which has red berries, has the advantage of not needing a pollinator. Gaultherias and pernettyas are good plants to combine with others, such as rhododendrons, which demand a lime-free, moist compost.

HEBE ☼ ▟

The shrubby veronicas are evergreen, the compact forms with neat foliage and dense flower spikes in summer. 'Red Edge' is a neat dwarf, about 16in/40cm in height, with a dense cover of grey-green leaves that are rimmed with red. The flowers are white. The so-called whipcord hebes have tiny leaves packed against the branches. *H. ochracea* 'James Stirling', generally under 1ft/30cm in height, is bright green in summer, turning bronze in winter.

HELIANTHEMUM ☼ ▜

The evergreen rock roses include many hybrids, mostly under 1ft/30cm in height but spreading freely, that flower prolifically throughout summer. Vivid colors include orange ('Ben Heckla' and 'Mrs Clay', also known as 'Fire Dragon'), deep pink ('Sudbury Gem') and reds ('Cerise Queen'). However, there are also soft pinks and yellow ('Wisley Pink' and 'Wisley Primrose') as well as white ('The Bride').

HEDERA ☼ ◐ ● ▟

The common ivy (*H. helix*) is a foliage plant of outstanding merit. It tolerates a wide range of conditions, can be grown as a trailer, a climber or as ground cover, and in its many cultivars offers a splendid choice of leaf shape, size and color. There are kinds with leaves that are crimped and waved, such as 'Cristata', others that are nearly pure yellow, for example 'Buttercup', and innumerable variegated kinds, such as the small-leaved 'Lutzii', which is mottled with cream, green and primrose. Almost all forms are worth

Reliable, fast-growing, almost indestructible: ivy is a standby of the windowbox.

growing. Ivy is one of the best trailers for windowboxes, building up impressive swags, 2–3ft/60–90cm long, of tightly clustered foliage.

JUNIPERUS ☀ ⬛

The dwarf column of *J. communis* 'Compressa' has become a cliché of miniature gardens. Several other good junipers, some of compact or spreading habit, are useful in long-term plantings. *J. squamata* 'Blue Star' is a bushy plant about 16in/40cm in height and width with dense foliage of a steely blue.

LAVANDULA ☀ ⬛

The lavenders have aromatic evergreen foliage as well as fragrant flowers. Short-growing kinds are suitable for containers and do well with other aromatic plants that like a free-draining compost. *L. angustifolia* 'Hidcote', with deep purplish flowers, and *L. a.* 'Nana Alba', with white flowers, can easily be kept under 2ft/60cm. A slightly larger plant with slender purple flower spikes is *L. × intermedia* 'Twickel Purple'. Trim annually.

LOTUS ☀ ⬛

A tall pot is better suited than a windowbox as a container for the cascading stems, as much as 2ft/60cm long, of *Lotus berthelotii*. The dense cover of narrow, silvery leaves makes this tender sub-shrub an attractive foliage plant but it also has curious beak-like scarlet flowers in summer. A well-grown specimen can be a useful and attractive centerpiece in a collection of pot-grown plants.

PINUS ☀ ⬛

Dwarf versions of the mountain pine (*P. mugo*) are suitable evergreen conifers to combine with rock garden plants. 'Humpy' slowly makes a rounded shrub to a height of about 16in/40cm with a dense cover of short needles. The needles of 'Ophir', which is a plant of similar size, turn bright gold during the winter months.

POTENTILLA ☀ ◑ ⬛

Although rather scruffy out of season, the shrubby potentillas make up for their appearance by producing small rose-like flowers in prodigious quantity throughout summer, and the deciduous foliage is often attractively silver grey. Compact cultivars of *P. fruticosa* that in height and spread are generally less than 2ft/60cm include: 'Kobold' – yellow flowers, bright green leaves; 'Manchu' (*P. f. mandschurica*) – white flowers, grey foliage; 'Pretty Polly' – salmon pink flowers; 'Royal Flush' – flowers sometimes semi-double, deep pink with a golden yellow center. Trim back lightly in spring.

RHODODENDRON ☀ ⬛

The dwarf evergreen rhododendrons are in the first rank of shrubs suitable for growing in containers in shady, lime-free positions. The foliage is pleasing all the year round, and the well-shaped flowers are borne profusely in spring or early summer. The following selection gives an idea of the wide color range available (old specimens may eventually exceed the dimensions given): 'Bluebird' – early, violet blue flowers; 'Dusty Miller' and 'Curlew' – 12 × 18in/30 × 45cm, yellow flowers over glossy green foliage; 'Dora Amateis' – 24 × 24in/60 × 60cm, white flowers spotted with green, dark green leaves; 'Elizabeth' – 24 × 30in/ 60 × 75cm, trumpet-shaped dark red flowers. The splendid hybrids developed from *R. yakushimanum* are generally less than 3ft/90cm in height but are better suited to pots or tubs than to windowboxes. Compact examples include: 'Bashful' – deep pink with reddish-brown blotch; 'Grumpy' – pale yellow tinged with pink; 'Sparkler' – crimson red.

ROSA

There is an increasingly wide choice of miniature roses, little bushes generally less than 1ft/30cm in height with leaves and flowers in perfect proportion.

Between these and the popular floribundas there are many new repeat-flowering roses that are less than 2ft/ 60cm in height. These are often marketed as 'patio roses'. Both categories can be grown satisfactorily in windowboxes and other containers, making a good display in summer.

The bare stems do not look attractive in winter, and it is best to move plants to a holding area when they are out of flower. There is an enormous color range to suit many different tastes.

My own preference if there is space for a reasonably large container is to use one of the new so-called ground-cover roses. They look attractive spilling over the container's edge, and many flower profusely over a long season. A good example is 'Snow Carpet', about 18in/ 45cm high and with a spread of about 3ft/90cm. The slightly fragrant double flowers are white.

SALIX

The willows include a few dwarf deciduous shrubs that mix well with rock-garden plants. *S. apoda*, for example, makes a gnarled shrub with a height and spread of up to 2ft/60cm. Male plants have attractive silver grey catkins in early spring. Even more gnarled is *S.* 'Boydii', which is very slow-growing but will eventually exceed 1ft/30cm. The prominently veined, ovate leaves are downy silver grey.

SANTOLINA

Most of the santolinas are too large for windowboxes. A useful exception is *S. chamaecyparissus nana*. This makes a compact bush of feathery foliage about 1ft/30cm in height. There are little yellow button flowers in midsummer. Trimming them off will help to keep the plant compact.

SKIMMIA

The glossy aromatic leaves of the skimmias are a useful long-term furnishing for windowboxes or containers in sun or light shade. Plants are slow-growing but will eventually make rounded shrubs more than 3ft/ 90cm in height and spread. Provided that there is a male plant to pollinate, female plants of *S. japonica*, such as 'Nymans', carry clusters of red holly-like berries from late summer until late winter. Although it has no berries, the male clone 'Rubella' is particularly ornamental on account of the red buds carried throughout winter, when the leaves are often tinged red. The buds open to white flowers in early spring. The compact *S. j. reevesiana* has hermaphrodite flowers and bears long-lasting fruit.

THUJA

The thujas are another group of evergreen conifers that have given rise to many dwarf cultivars, some of which are suitable for windowboxes. *T. occidentalis* 'Danica' makes a neat, rounded bush about 20in/50cm in height and diameter. The dark green summer foliage takes on attractive bronze coloring in winter.

VINCA

The lesser periwinkle (*V. minor*) is a sprawling shrub, up to 6in/15cm high but often with a spread of more than 30in/75cm. The simple but prettily shaped flowers, in shades of blue and purple or white, are carried for several months from early spring. The evergreen leaves are glossy dark green but the variegated cultivars, such as the yellow splashed 'Aureovariegata', are useful for brightening a permanent planting scheme. The periwinkles are not fussy plants; indeed their vigor may well need to be checked.

HERBS, VEGETABLES AND FRUIT

This selection is tailored to gardening in the confined space of a windowbox, but a much wider selection of useful plants can be easily grown if you have a small yard or patio where there is room for pots, tubs and growbags.

BASIL ☀ ▣
A choice kitchen herb, common or sweet basil (*Ocimum basilicum*) is a tender annual that needs a sheltered position as well as sun. Pinch back frequently, removing flower heads as soon as they appear, to keep plants leafy and under 2ft/60cm in height. A red-leaved form, also well flavored, makes a lovely contrast with green herbs. Easier for pots but milder in flavor, the dwarf Greek basil (*O. minimum*), which has narrow leaves, makes a bushy plant usually less than 1ft/30cm high.

BORAGE ☀ ▣
An annual herb, borage (*Borago officinalis*) has hairy, cucumber-flavored leaves and starry blue flowers. Old plants can grow to 3ft/90cm but it is the young leaves that are used in salads and drinks. Sowing a few seeds at intervals from mid-spring until midsummer will provide suitable plants, best grown in pots, that can be discarded when they become too large.

CABBAGE ☀ ▣
The cabbages to grow in containers are the ornamental kinds, which make splendid rosettes of often frilled leaves in pinks, purples, cream, white and blue-green. These annuals are edible but they are best left to please the eye, especially for autumn and winter effect,

when cold temperatures intensify their color. Pot-grown plants are fairly readily available. To raise cabbages from seed, sow in spring.

CHIVES ☀ ✹ ▣
Among the most useful perennial herbs to grow near the kitchen, chives (*Allium schoenoprasum*) are easy plants for containers but need frequent watering in dry weather. The grey-green tubular leaves grow to about 10in/25cm. Though the starry pink flowers that appear in summer are very attractive, they should be removed in order to maintain a supply of leaves for cutting. The flavor of Chinese chives (*A. tuberosum*) gives them their alternative name of garlic chives. Also perennial, these have flat leaves and starry white flowers. In their second and subsequent years they can grow to 20in/50cm.

HYSSOP ☀ ▣
Even the young leaves of hyssop (*Hyssopus officinalis*) are too bitter to use generously as a kitchen herb. This evergreen shrubby perennial makes an attractive aromatic addition to plants that like free-draining soil. The stems, up to 18in/45cm tall, are densely clothed in narrow leaves and carry purplish flowers in late summer.

LETTUCE ☀ ✹ ▣
The most suitable lettuces for growing in containers are the loose-leaf 'salad bowl' types. The red and green oak-leaved lettuces are especially pretty and, if only a few leaves are picked at a time, they will remain attractive over a long season. Lettuces are annuals and to get

the kinds you want it may be necessary to raise plants yourself from seed.

MINT ☀ ✹ ● ▣
The mints (*Mentha*) are refreshingly aromatic perennial herbs, useful for container gardening as they will tolerate shade. To do well, however, they need a moisture-retentive compost. Both the common mint (*M. spicata*) and the apple mint (*M. × rotundifolia*) need pinching back to keep them under 2ft/60cm. Several variegated mints make bold foliage plants. For a cool combination of white and green, choose *M. suaveolens* 'Variegata', which grows to 10in/25cm. For warmer tones of creamy yellow and green, the choice should be *M. × gentilis* 'Variegata', which can reach 18in/45cm.

PARSLEY ☀ ✹ ▣
Curled parsley, which has mossy, dark green leaves and grows up to 20in/50cm high, is an indispensable herb and a very ornamental foliage plant, whether mixed with other herbs or grown with flowers. When growing it in small quantities, buy young plants rather than sowing seed of this biennial, which sometimes germinates erratically. Italian or plain-leaved parsley is also good in containers. It makes a less substantial plant but has a particularly good flavor.

ROSEMARY ☀ ▣
Rosemary (*Rosmarinus officinalis*) is among the most refined of aromatic shrubs. Although many forms of this evergreen shrub are too tall for window gardening, some are, fortunately, low-growing sprawlers. 'McConnell's Blue', for example, is only about 10in/25cm

high. More tender but also prostrate is the hybrid *R. × lavandulaceus*. The blue flowers of these rosemaries, an attractive bonus in spring, often last well into summer.

RUE ☼ ▽

A pungently aromatic and bitter herb, rue (*Ruta graveolens*) is now mainly grown as an ornamental, 'Jackman's Blue' being one of the best shrubby grey-blue foliage plants for containers. Grow in gritty well-drained soil and pinch back to keep under 2ft/60cm. Trim plants in mid-spring.

SAGE ☼ ▽

An evergreen shrubby herb, common sage (*Salvia officinalis*) has textured,

Where daily care can be given, lettuces and tomatoes are both productive and decorative.

grey-green leaves that make a good contrast for more showy plants that also like free-draining soil. The purple-leaved form, 'Purpurascens', gives weight to a silver planting scheme. Both these need frequent pinching back to keep them under 2ft/60cm. Less vigorous are the golden variegated form 'Icterina' and the blotched 'Tricolor', which has cream and purplish pink markings overlaying green.

STRAWBERRY ☼ ◑ ▽

Strawberries can be attractive plants for containers, but a single windowbox will yield only a small crop. The alpine strawberries, such as 'Baron Solemacher', are perhaps a better choice than the normal large-fruited kinds. The latter grow about 10in/25cm high and their attractive leaves make them useful foliage plants to combine with ornamentals.

THYME ☼ ▽

Piquant kitchen herbs, many of the thymes (*Thymus*) have attractive foliage and flower heads; generally pink to purple, the flowers appear in dense clusters in early summer. These compact shrubs, rarely more than 16in/40cm tall and sometimes ground-hugging, are good candidates for troughs or containers, combined with other herbs or ornamentals that also like free-draining soil. An aromatic family collection is another possibility. As well as the common thyme (*T. vulgaris*), look for lemon thyme (*T. × citriodorus*), which has attractive variegated and golden forms, 'Doone Valley', which has handsomely gold-splashed leaves, and selected forms of the wild thyme (*T. serpyllum*), such as *T. s. coccinea*, whose dark green leaves are smothered in summer with rich crimson flowers.

TOMATO ☼ ▼

Although a window space can give only a small crop of tomatoes, the fruits are very attractive as they ripen from green to red. The compact tomatoes that have been developed for container-growing in a limited space, such as the F$_1$ cultivars 'Totem' and 'Tumbler', are better suited to growing in pots than in windowboxes. These are not, however, easily bought as young plants, and it may be worth sharing a packet of seed if you are raising your own. They need to be started under glass. Harden off young plants before moving them outdoors permanently in late spring or early summer. Tomatoes need a rich compost, regular feeding throughout summer and a copious supply of water.

Growing Windowbox Plants

With an understanding of a few basic requirements, the novice can easily achieve plant results to match those of experienced gardeners.

CONTAINERS

Containers must be of sufficient size to hold enough compost to meet the needs of plants, have drainage holes so that water does not stagnate and eventually drown the plants, and be raised up off a flat surface so that water can run straight off, not creep into cracks and crevices in the wall or sill. Stand boxes or pots on wedges or feet about 1in/2.5cm high, especially when using drip trays, which simply hold the water. The smallest practical size for a box is 6in/15cm wide and 8in/20cm deep.

Always make windowboxes secure. You can tap in wooden wedges at each end to hold it firmly, tie wires between screws on the wall or windowframe, or fit a bar across the front of the sill.

Where a sill itself is unsuitable, it may be possible to mount a box below it on brackets. These must be firmly secured to both wall and box.

COMPOSTS

Plants grown in containers need specially formulated composts, free of weed seed, pests and diseases, that give good anchorage, contain a balanced supply of nutrients and retain moisture without becoming sodden and airless.

There are two main kinds of ready-prepared composts, loam-based and soilless. John Innes potting composts are soil-based. The name is not a brand but refers to the formulation of a mixture consisting of loam, peat and sand, together with a base fertilizer. Their richness varies according to the amount of base fertilizer they contain. John Innes No. 1 is for slow-growing plants, such as alpines. No. 2, a richer mixture, suits a wide range of plants, including most of those used in summer schemes. No. 3, even richer, is for shrubs and fast-growing plants, such as tomatoes. There are also John Innes formulations for seed and ericaceous composts. The ericaceous compost contains no chalk and is therefore suitable for lime-hating plants.

There is less standardization in the formulation of the soilless composts, in which peat is often combined with other inert materials such as sand, perlite or vermiculite. Environmental concern has led to the use of several peat substitutes, including coir. Although many of these composts are acidic, some contain too much chalk to be suitable for lime-hating plants. The information on the packet should make clear the range of plants for which they are appropriate. As a rule, soilless composts are cheaper than loam-based kinds and are clean to handle. Their lightness can be an advantage too, for example in a windowbox supported by brackets. The nutrients they contain, however, are used up relatively quickly, and regular feeding is needed to maintain healthy growth. Unless they have been treated with a wetting agent, they do not take up water readily once they have been allowed to dry out. More than light firming at planting can cause compaction and waterlogging.

For short-term schemes it is a matter of personal choice whether you use a loam-based or a soilless compost. Provided the compost is kept to the desired level, it can be used for a succession of plantings, though after a year it should be discarded and the containers scrubbed out and re-filled.

For long-term schemes my choice would always be loam-based composts because they provide better anchorage and a longer-lasting supply of nutrients. Plants may be left in the same container for five or six years if the compost is rejuvenated annually. To do this, scrape away the top 2–3in/5–7.5cm, and replace with fresh compost containing a slow-release fertilizer.

MULCHES

The application of a mulch can give a neat finish to windowboxes and other containers. For shrubs and the larger perennials a layer of pulverized bark about 2in/5cm deep is ideal. This will minimize splash, help to conserve moisture, and discourage the growth of weeds. A layer of stone chippings about 1in/2.5cm deep is more suitable for rock-garden plants.

PLANTING

Planting is the simplest and, to me, the most satisfying part of window gardening, particularly enjoyable because one can afford to flout the normal recommendations for planting densities that apply to the open garden. Crowd plants in, but not so that there is insufficient room for their rootballs. A windowbox full of moist compost and plants can be heavy and unwieldy, so if possible fill and plant the box in its display position.

With adequate drainage holes and purpose-built brackets to hold them secure, these windowboxes fit the bill.

soilless composts than with those that are loam-based. As a last step, water the whole container thoroughly.

WATER SUPPLY AND DRAINAGE

Most plants will collapse quickly if not regularly watered, but they will also die if the compost is waterlogged and airless. A well-formulated compost is moisture-retentive but allows free drainage and will suit the requirements of a wide range of plants. For plants that like an open and free-draining compost add horticultural grit to standard formulations. Increasing the water retentiveness of composts in containers is more difficult. One way is to incorporate polymers – available as plant-watering crystals – into the compost at planting time; but on the whole the special requirements of moisture-loving plants usually have to be met by frequent watering.

The holes in the bottom of containers must allow excess water to drain freely. A layer of coarse material about 1in/5cm deep in the base of the container, consisting of clay crocks (broken fragments of terracotta pots), expanded clay pellets, coarse gravel or pea shingle will help drainage.

Watering is best done in early morning or in the evening, because in bright sunshine splashes on leaves often result in scorching. A swan-necked attachment to a hose can be useful in watering windowboxes above ground-floor level. Test the compost before watering by plunging a finger below the surface. Overwatering can cause plants to sicken and rot. If the compost is nearly dry, water the surface of the

It is a good idea to position plants provisionally in their original pots since the more they are moved about the more chance there is of roots being damaged. In mixed plantings put in shrubs before perennials and short-term plants. Bulbs that are to grow through other plants need to go in at an early stage. They can be planted deeper than

is often recommended, and to achieve a really dense display you can plant one layer above another.

When firming compost round plants, remember to use a lighter touch with compost, not the leaves. Loam-based compducts are best watered thoroughly, until water runs out of the drainage holes. Soilless composts are better given smaller amounts of water but more frequently. Do not assume that rain will adequately water containers; of the little rain that reaches a windowbox, most will run straight off the leaves.

Busy gardeners might consider a micro-irrigation system, in which a main pipe feeds drippers that keep the compost moist without saturating it. Alternatively, water-absorbent polymers added to the compost will provide a reservoir without the compost itself becoming waterlogged.

Feeding

The density of container-planting means that heavy demands are made on the nutrients contained in the compost. Some of the nutrients get washed out when plants are watered, and growth will suffer if the supply is not boosted by the addition of fertilizers.

There are two main kinds of fertilizer suitable for window gardening. Those that are fast-acting but effective for a relatively short period are available in liquid form or as powders that are mixed with water before being applied. Those that release their nutrients slowly over a long period are normally applied in granule or tablet form. Chemical fertilizers are easy and clean to use and dominate the market, but there are also a number of organic fertilizers, such as slow-acting bonemeal, and liquid feeds derived from seaweed.

Short-term planting schemes, particularly using soilless composts, are best fed regularly, with liquid fertilizers applied every seven to ten days throughout the growing season. Food crops also need generous feeding, and fruit-bearing is encouraged by the high potassium content of liquid fertilizers designed for tomato growing.

Slow-release fertilizers are ideal for long-term schemes. A single application at planting and annually when the compost is rejuvenated will be sufficient for most shrubs and perennials. Alpines and most rock-garden plants need no more than a light annual dressing of bonemeal in spring.

Pinching Out, Trimming and Pruning

Provided that suitable plants have been selected for containers, there is usually not much need for pruning and training. With some plants, for example fuchsias and coleus, it is worthwhile encouraging bushy growth while they are still young. Pinching out the growing tips encourages the sideshoots below to develop.

Most compact shrubs, including evergreen dwarf conifers, need no pruning at all beyond the removal of diseased and damaged wood. Others may need light pruning to remove wayward shoots. These should be taken out in a way that does not disfigure the plant's natural growth and overall shape, if possible by cutting back a stem to a junction with another stem.

Most evergreens need only light pruning, preferably between mid- and late spring. A few evergreens, including lavenders, lose their compact shape unless hard pruned in spring. The summer- and autumn-flowering heathers also need to be trimmed in spring to prevent them becoming leggy.

Prune deciduous shrubs that flower in spring or early summer as soon as flowering has finished. Most deciduous shrubs that flower later can be pruned during the dormant season. Roses fall into this category. Cut out dead, diseased and weak growth and inward-growing stems. The remaining stems should then be cut back just above outward-facing buds to a height of 4–6in/10–15cm.

Without annual pruning the shape of topiary specimens would soon be lost. Trim in late summer or early autumn, removing virtually the whole of the previous season's growth. Regular deadheading, in effect a form of pruning, is an important means of prolonging the flowering season.

Winter Protection

Tender and half-hardy plants that are to be kept going from one year to the next (even if only as material for cuttings) must be lifted in autumn and kept in frost-free conditions throughout the winter. Other plants that are hardy in the open garden may suffer if the rootball becomes frozen, and containers themselves can suffer frost damage in low temperatures; wrapping them in materials such as hessian (burlap) and straw will protect them.

Raising Plants

Although many gardeners are happy to buy plants as they need them, others feel they have cheated unless they raise their own. Propagation is not difficult;

with small-scale gardening the problem is often a shortage of space in a well-lit area under cover. A heated propagator that will fit on a windowsill is probably the best answer if you want to raise plants for short-term summer displays. Even a seed tray inside a polythene bag will give good results in a warm, well-lit room with only slight fluctuations in temperature. Sow thinly so that seedlings do not have to compete with one another. When they have developed their first true leaves they can be individually lifted and planted in trays filled with potting compost. As they develop they must be hardened off by exposing them gradually to outdoor conditions over about a week.

Tender shrubby plants such as fuchsias and pelargoniums can be overwintered in frost-free conditions, and healthy young shoots can be taken as cuttings in early spring. To maintain the warm, moist conditions necessary for rooting, make a tent of a clear plastic bag over the pot, tying it round the top. Once the cuttings have rooted, harden them off before planting outdoors.

PROBLEMS

Much of window gardening is smooth sailing. You should, however, examine plants carefully before buying them and discard those harboring pests or showing symptoms of disease, such as distorted growth or discolored foliage.

The scale of the window garden makes it easy to detect problems at an early stage. Whenever possible, chemical solutions should be avoided: many large pests can be picked off, and a spray of soapy water can be effective

against aphids. These and other sucking pests do, however, carry diseases that weaken and eventually kill plants, and I normally use a contact insecticide to control them. Slugs and snails can be so destructive on such a scale that I resort to chemical warfare against them.

Many fungal diseases can be avoided by planting resistant cultivars, and

although many gardeners take preventive measures by spraying regularly with a systemic fungicide, I prefer to use a chemical spray only when the problem presents itself.

With an appropriate choice of plants and a little attention to their care, a glorious summer display is easy to achieve.

Index

Acknowledgments

The publisher would like to thank the following photographers and organizations for their kind permission to reproduce the photographs in this book:

1 Juliette Wade/Garden Picture Library; 2 Michèle Lamontagne; 4–5 Roland Beaufre/Agence Top; 6 IMP/William Mason; 7 Lynne Brotchie/Garden Picture Library; 8 Susan Witney; 9 Marijke Heuff (Nelly Christiaans); 10 John Neubauer/Garden Picture Library; 11 Jerry Harpur; 12 David Joyce; 13 Brigitte Thomas; 14 Jerry Harpur (Designer: Susie Ind); 15 left Michael Boys/Boys Syndication; 15 right Neil Holmes; 16 Michèle Lamontagne; 17 Jerry Harpur; 22 Juliette Wade/Garden Picture Library; 18 Jacqui Hurst/Boys Syndication; 19 Georges Lévêque; 24 above Camera Press; 24 below Clive Nichols (Designer: Anthony Noel); 25 Neil Holmes; 26 Ann Kelly/Garden Picture Library; 27 left Marijke Heuff (Mr and Mrs Gentis); 27 right Clive Nichols (Designer: Anthony Noel); 30 S&O Mathews; 31 Jerry Harpur/Elizabeth Whiting and Associates; 32 left Jacqui Hurst/Boys Syndication; 32 right Linda Burgess/Garden Picture Library; 33 Jacqui Hurst/Boys Syndication; 34 Andrew Lawson; 35 Michèle Lamontagne; 36 David Joyce; 37 above Brigitte Thomas; 37 below Jerry Harpur (Designer: Susie Ind); 40 Andrew Lawson; 41 Marie O'Hara/Elizabeth Whiting and Associates; 42 Gary Rogers; 43 left Eric Crichton; 43 right Jacqui Hurst/Boys Syndication; 44 Andrew Lawson; 45 Jon Bouchier/Garden Picture Library; 48 Jerry Harpur (Designer: Peter Ottaway); 50 left W.A. Lord; 50 right Michèle Lamontagne; 51 John Neubauer/Garden Picture Library; 52 Linda Burgess/Garden Picture Library; 53 above W.A. Lord; 54 Linda Burgess/Garden Picture Library; 55 Marianne Majerus; 56 Karen Bussolini; 57 below Jerry Pavia/Garden Picture Library; 60 Karen Bussolini; 61 Gary Rogers; 62 Jacqui Hurst/Boys Syndication; 63 above Brigitte Thomas; 63 below Marijke Heuff; 64 John Glover; 65 Michèle Lamontagne; 66 Marijke Heuff (Designer: Ada Roest); 67 Marijke Heuff (Designer: Anthony Noel); 72 Clive Nichols; 73 Michèle Lamontagne; 75 Jerry Harpur; 77 S&O Mathews; 79 David Joyce; 81 Camera Press; 82 Jacqui Hurst/Boys Syndication; 84 Andrew Lawson; 86 Linda Burgess/Garden Picture Library; 89 Eric Crichton; 91 Gary Rogers; 93 Andrew Lawson.

The following photographs were taken by Pia Tryde and styled by Juliette Wade: 20–21 (styled by Jane Newdick), 23, 28–9, 38–9, 46–7, 49, 53 below, 57 above, 58–9, 68–9, 70–1.

Index compiled by Indexing Specialists, Hove, East Sussex, England BN3 2DJ.

The publishers would like to thank the following people for making their houses available for location photography: Isabelle Bowden, Stephen and Sally Clarke, Jennifer Humber, Sue Loughnan, and Jane Newdick.